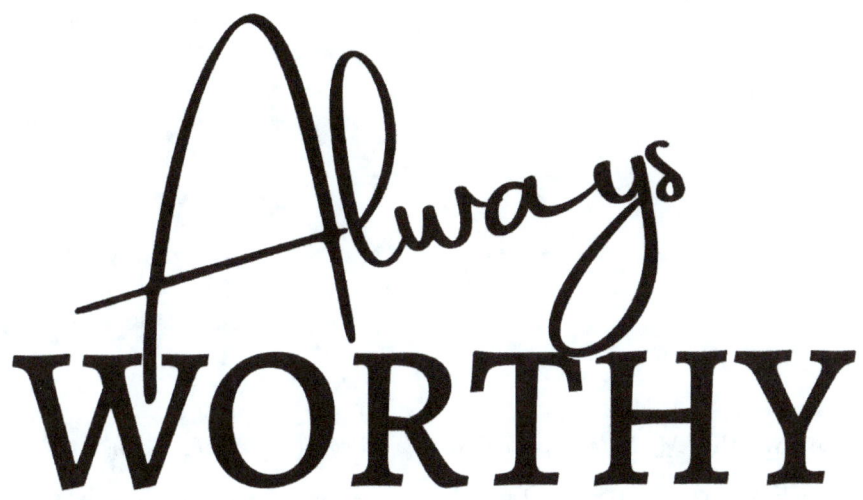

Always WORTHY

MY BADASS SPIRITUAL REBELLION FINDING MYSELF AFTER LOSING MY MOM

Dr. Emy Tafelski

"The healing was in the surrender, not in the control, in the letting it in, not in the ignoring it and pushing it away."

–Emy Tafelski

CONTENTS

Dedication vii

Acknowledgments ix

Introduction xi

Profound Loss xvi

Interlude xxi

Chapter 1: Untethered 1

Chapter 2: Comfort 17

Chapter 3: Guides Along the Way 35

Chapter 4: Healing 43

Different Types of Healing 44

How Can I Have a Birthday but Not a Mother?. 48

Birthday Retreat 50

Womb Cleansing Ritual 56

Women's Temple Facilitator Training 58

Other Trainings 60

Lived Spirituality 61

Chapter 5: Surrender **65**

Existential Aloneness and the Energetic Umbilical Cord. . . 66

Playing Small 68

The Feminine 70

Soul Parts 71

Sexual Trauma 72

Chapter 6: Dismantling the Physical Box **81**

One Year Since Mom's Death 86

Back to Work 88

Chapter 7: Choosing Authenticity... Again **91**

Ch-Ch-Ch-Changes 92

What Do I Truly Want? 92

Chapter 8: A Recap **97**

The Soul's Tapestry 98

Wholeness 99

Threads Unwoven 99

Patriarchy 100

Disordered Eating 101

Threads Rewoven 102

Soul Parts 103

The Feminine 104

The Always Worthy 105

The Body 105

Conclusion . . . . **.107**

About the Author . . . . **.113**

DEDICATION

This book is dedicated to my mom and all the women who've come before me who've lived the lives they've been told to live rather than the lives that were true to them and their hearts and souls. May we all find our way to unapologetic authenticity and wholeness.

ACKNOWLEDGMENTS

I adapted this work from my doctoral dissertation; thus, my acknowledgments align with the ones I crafted for that work.

I have never thrived when I've been put in a box that defines who I should be versus allowed to flow as who I am authentically. I am grateful that when I began this work in graduate school, I had a dissertation committee that allowed me the freedom to be me and to follow my intuition in the research process. They encouraged me to rest into who I am and what was needed to create the original work within me.

Without their guidance, my dissertation would not have been as deep and meaningful as it was, this book would not have had as deep of a foundation to pull from, and I would have been less formed and less whole as a result of the entire process. The original dissertation and, subsequently, this book allowed me to write myself back into being, and I am forever grateful.

I am immensely grateful to the healers who have stood by my side and guided my return to wholeness. They held the space, organized the rituals and ceremonies, and held the sacred container that allowed me to heal and develop my process. I could not have done this without them and their light and teachings.

Though this work is lengthy, I don't have enough words to express my gratitude for my husband, Greg. He sacrificed so much so that I could complete my doctorate and this book. He challenges me when I need it, lifts me when I fall, encourages me when I hit a wall, and so much more. There is no one I would rather be on this journey with than you.

I also want to thank my soul sister, Dawn McDaniel. I have no idea how I would have done this without her! It is amazing to think that we only met in our first semester of doctoral work, yet she is such an integral part of my life. I think we have known each other for lifetimes. I would not have been able to do this without her support, occasional kicks in the butt, all of our talks, and our intentional ceremonies.

There are so many others who have supported me along the way: friends, teachers, and family, and I am grateful for them all.

I am also grateful for the support of Goddess. She held me when I crumbled and gave me a scaffolding within which to rebuild and become. She sees me, knows me, and values me always. It is my honor to embody my Goddess-given mission of increasing authenticity in the world.

Finally, I am grateful to my cats, China Cat Sunflower and Cleopatra, for keeping me company while I spent hours writing the original dissertation and for letting me know when it was time to quit by sitting on my arms and making it impossible to continue.

INTRODUCTION

Have you ever wondered how much of you is actually you? Most of us don't think about this. We assume that who we are is, in fact, who we are. I learned differently when my mom died, despite a lifelong dedication to my personal growth, spiritual development, and embodied authenticity.

Following her death, I embarked on a year-long healing journey that, at its heart, was a deep voyage into all of the threads that make me me. What I was shocked to find was that I was made up of threads woven into my soul by my mom and the trauma that she carried around with her; by messages I internalized from the family around me, most of them messages that didn't serve me; by threads from my own trauma and survival mechanisms; and most importantly and impactfully, woven insidiously throughout my soul were the threads of patriarchy.

I want to be clear that when I talk about patriarchy, it is a *system*. I do not refer to men, who are bound by the chains of patriarchy as well, but in different ways. Oxford Learner's Dictionaries defines a system as "a set of principles or procedures according to which something is done; an organized framework or method."[1] Patriar-

---

[1] "Oxford Advanced Learner's Dictionary," Oxford Learner's Dictionaries, accessed January 22, 2024, https://www.oxfordlearnersdictionaries.com/us/definition/english/.

chy is the organized system that dictates, in many ways, how we behave and what we feel or don't feel. It is a system that privileges men, mostly white men. It looks down on women and women's perceived ways of being.

In the system of patriarchy, men hold substantially more positions of power than women. It is a society where the core values deemed normal are generally traits associated with how men are viewed. "Because patriarchy is male-identified and male-centered, women and the work they do tend to be devalued, if not made invisible, and women are routinely repressed in their development as human beings through neglect and discrimination in schools and occupational hiring, development, promotion, and rewards."[2] Women consistently feel less-than, unworthy, and as though they have to prove their worth and value by productivity or service. This thread of unworthiness was a big driving force throughout my life.

Patriarchy is a thread woven throughout this book as it is the culture within which I (and most of us, if not all) was raised. As such, it weaves its threads throughout my soul's tapestry. I focused a large part of this healing journey on noticing and unweaving the threads of patriarchy that I didn't even realize were part of my framework and directed my behavior and, specifically, my survival mechanisms.

Throughout this book, you'll read a lot about how I survived as a youngster, teen, and young adult in different ways by doing things to get the love I desperately needed rather than believing that I was loved and lovable because I was me. This is patriarchy at work, compounded by my family's cultural message of not being good enough.

---

[2] Allan G. Johnson, essay, in The Gender Knot: Unraveling Our Patriarchal Legacy (Philadelphia, PA: Temple University Press, 2014), p. 15.

Though patriarchy's reach is far and insidious, I think most people don't think about it daily. For deep soul healing, however, it is imperative that we become more conscious of what forces outside of ourselves guide our behavior and that we unweave those from our tapestry to become more whole and authentic. Women, like me and you, raised within the system of patriarchy, also devalue the feminine within ourselves and around us and are thus cut off and separated from this part of ourselves.

As women, we must reclaim and revalue the feminine within ourselves to move toward a deeper relationship with wholeness and authenticity. During this journey of healing and alchemy that follows, I had to do the work of reclaiming and embodying the feminine within me, of honoring it and revering it, of highlighting and lifting it up so that I could be guided and rest into it instead of cutting it off and shoving it in a box to be forgotten.

Something important to know about me is that I am a deeply spiritual person heavily engaged in my own Divine Feminine embodied spiritual practice. Divine Feminine spirituality sees the Divine with a female face, the Goddess, The Great Mother. Divine Feminine spirituality is relational. It values and affirms women's ways of being in the world. Divine Feminine spirituality allows me to connect with a powerful force, Goddess, who is like me rather than an imposing male God, the father.

While it is sometimes difficult to define Divine Feminine and Goddess spirituality, I can tell you what it means to me and how I live it. My spirituality is a major theme throughout this book. It was and is a guiding force for my life and any healing journey I embark on. For me, Goddess spirituality is an embodied practice. It comes through me, resides in me, works me. It, or She (Goddess), is not separate from me or my experience. She is available to me and with me always. It's okay if your beliefs differ from mine, but this was a major factor in my healing that you will hear a lot about in the pages ahead.

Since patriarchy has affected the religious foundation of much of the world, my dedication to Goddess spirituality is in itself a step on the journey of change and revolution. It is bucking the system that I am constrained by. It's breaking out of the box of what I've been told is allowed, expected, and correct—worship of God, the father.

North American culture was built on a masculine religious founda-tion.[3] This masculine religious foundation helped to create a culture of male domination.[4] While it is true that not all dominant religious traditions actively work to oppress women, and some even allow women to serve as pastors or religious leaders, it is also true that religions built on a God–as–male foundation impact the creation of society, gender roles, and sense of Self.[5] This devalues the feminine. The invisibility that we, as women, face in male-dominated reli-gions contributes to a spiritual wounding of the feminine, which shows up in girls and women as they grow.[6]

This framework has formed how I show up in the world sexually and just generally as a woman. It has woven throughout my soul

---

[3] Rosemary Radford Ruether, *Goddesses and the Divine Feminine: A Western Religious History* (University of California Press, 2006).

[4] K.J. Grijalva, "Reclaiming the erotic self: Goddess spirituality and recovery from rape," Doc-toral dissertation, Institute of Transpersonal Psychology (Publication No. 3408065), 2010.

[5] Stephanie Amanda Melmed, "Source of Connection, Strength and Identity : An Exploration of How a Belief in the Divine as Feminine Affects Women's Internal and External Relation-ships," Smith ScholarWorks, 2007, https://scholarworks.smith.edu/theses/423/.

[6] Jamie Funderburk and Mary Fukuyama, "Feminism, Multiculturalism, and Spirituality: Convergent and Divergent Forces in Psychotherapy," Taylor & Francis Online Women & Therapy, September 24, 2008, https://msesiom.demo.elsevierpure.com/en/publications/feminism-multiculturalism-and-spirituality-convergent-and-diverge-2.

threads of feeling not good enough, unworthy, less than. It's led to being a people pleaser, to doing and being things that weren't true to who I am. It has pulled me far afield from my authentic self. Living life far from my inner truth left me anxious, uncertain, trapped, and, at times, suffering from chronic illness.

What if you could do internal work to see those chains wrapped around you, pulling you down, holding you back, getting in your way? What if you could unwrap them, break them, and become free, free to be you, all of you, like you were when you were a child swinging from the monkey bars before the world told you who you should be?

This book chronicles my journey of breaking those chains, of taking my shattered, grief-ridden soul, and alchemizing my pain into unapologetic authenticity and deep connection to spirit. It is the story of unweaving the threads from my soul's tapestry that don't serve me and aren't mine to carry and reweaving and reclaiming those parts of me that were lost or cut off in my effort to fit into a box of lovability.

While this wasn't the first time in my life that I had taken my lost and broken soul and deepened into a more true version of myself, it was the most profound, the most long-lasting, and the one that helped me finally develop a system that can be shared with you so that you too can learn who you truly are and live from a place of inner truth. Everyone deserves to live life from a place of inner truth and authenticity, to break free from the chains and boxes that family trauma, personal trauma, and the system around you saddle you with. My mission is to help you do just that, using my journey and story as examples.

Profound Loss

On October 31, 2017, my mom lost her nine-year battle with pancreatic cancer. I was 42. I wasn't a child, but I still felt too young to lose my mom. We were a team, and though my parents were still together, my father wasn't as present, involved, or engaged as my mother.

We explored the world together and moved through it as a unit until I moved to a different state at 28. We were best friends. I was shattered by the loss, even though it wasn't unexpected. In some ways, I was surprised by how much it impacted me. There was a story in my head that said that this is the natural order. Parents typically die before their children, so I "shouldn't" be so impacted by her death.

But that wasn't my reality. I was gutted. There was such a profound emptiness inside my being. I felt like there had been some kind of tether connecting me to my mother, and that tether was no longer attached to anything. It was floating freely, unanchored, and drifting in the air without purchase, without substance, like dust on the wind.

I realized that I no longer knew who I was. It felt like this thread, this tether, had been a scaffolding holding me together, and without it, I disappeared. Had you told me before Mom's death that this was how it would impact me, I never would have believed you. I've spent a lot of time on my healing journey throughout my life, since the age of 16 when I first went to a therapist. I'd dedicated most of this journey to deepening my authenticity and becoming more of who I really was, so how could this death, this trauma, shatter so much of my Self? How could this loss unravel me to such a degree that I needed to rediscover who I was in the world without a mother?

This was the beginning of a journey of healing: of releasing and reclaiming, anchoring, and becoming whole and authentically me in a deeper and more profound way than I ever thought possible.

Trauma isn't a new experience for me. Unfortunately, it has been an almost constant companion since I was very young. I have also experienced losses: the loss of important beings in my life, the loss of ideas of my Self, the loss of parts of my soul to trauma, the loss of close loved ones, and the loss of health, life goals, and plans. I have had no choice but to commit to my healing journey throughout adulthood. The other option would have been to live as a shadow of myself, asleep, broken, lost. That wasn't really an option at all.

My trauma history and the incredible impact that my first therapist had on me led me to pursue a career as a holistic, soul-focused psychotherapist. I truly felt that this was my calling: to help people in their journey of healing and authenticity. Through this journey of healing from the loss of my mom, my work in the world has drastically shifted focus. My passion and mission have deepened and expanded into helping people step into the power of their unapologetic authenticity and, as part of this process, unweave patriarchy from their soul's tapestry.

I engaged in this healing journey as a participant, a researcher, and an observer. Mom died during my first semester of doctoral work; thus, all my research shifted to make space for my healing journey, to research it, and to write about it as I went through it.

Goddess was a driving force behind all of this work. She whispered in my ear about my mission in the world as a warrior for authenticity and worthiness, both authenticity and worthiness being spiritual healing and practice. It wasn't until I could fully study my journey that I began to appreciate all I had done and see how to transform it into an offering to guide others to their deepest authentic selves.

In studying my healing journey, I've distilled it down to create a process of soul-deep healing and transformation for others, called Soul Weaver™, that mirrors my process of healing described in this book.

While the entire process has four phases, the two most important are release and reclaim. These two form the bulk of what you'll read about in the following pages, though I'll also include some information on the other two: attune and anchor.

In the first phase, attune, I turned my attention toward my soul's tapestry; I let all of my feelings be present, I slowed down enough to feel my feelings, and I zoomed out for the larger perspective of my soul. During this phase, I was attuned to the healing portal and made the conscious decision to step through the portal and into the healing matrix, dedicating myself to deep healing.

Activating the healing matrix allowed me a deeper, brighter perception of my soul's tapestry, and I could see its different threads leading me to phase 2, release. During release, I sifted through the different threads that made up my tapestry, noticing what was discordant, what didn't belong to me, the threads that came from trauma passed down within my family, and threads that were woven in by the culture around me, specifically patriarchy.

I did the work of unweaving these threads and releasing them, freeing them from my tapestry, which then became more authentically me, leading directly to phase 3, reclaim. During reclaim, I paid attention to the holes in my soul's tapestry, areas where I lost parts due to trauma or intentionally jettisoned parts of my soul or Self because I received messages that it wasn't alright to be who I really am. I reclaimed these lost soul parts and rewove them into my soul's tapestry again, or maybe for the first time. Woven throughout this phase was a reclaiming of the feminine within me.

Once I did this, I shifted into anchor, phase 4, where I tightened the tapestry weave and anchored it into my being, more whole and authentic than before. I also learned how to keep coming back to these threads when needed because, let's face it, healing isn't linear! Sometimes, lifelong wounds pop up differently, and I'll need to attend to them again.

My engagement with my healing journey is a large part of the mechanism that has allowed me to successfully meet my clients where they are in their pain and healing journey. Having journeyed from untethered, disconnected, and lost to reconnected, anchored, and whole, I am intimately familiar with the process of healing transformation after a realization that you don't know who you are in the world, the knowledge that you've been living by some script created outside of you and not following your inner truth.

My mission is to bring that knowledge to you through this book and my coaching programs, to increase your authenticity and lead you straight to living a life grounded in your true essence, a life of "Hell, yes!"

INTERLUDE

This book was partially written and adapted from my doctoral dissertation, "Reweaving the Tapestry of the Self: An Evocative Autoethnography Dissertation Study Exploring the Healing Journey Following Mother Loss."

In this book, I will take you with me on the journey of healing from the time of my mother's death to the present day. The story begins right before my mom died. I intend for you, the reader, to experience my journey home to myself and my unapologetic authenticity with me and to come out the other side feeling hopeful and fired up for your journey home to your Self.

Chapter 1

UNTETHERED

We took funeral clothes for our visit. Why? I'm not sure. Intuition, I guess. I was driving in my car to visit a friend, and the phone rang. I looked down at the dash to see who was calling. "Dad" scrolled across the screen. I was puzzled at first and then worried. Seeing his name as the caller created a pit of anxiety and confusion in my belly. He did not call me often. It was my mom who usually called, my mom whose life was intimately entwined with my own in ways that most therapists would likely call enmeshed. (Since I'm a therapist, I'm qualified to make this assessment!) In fact, it was even more entwined than I knew at the time. I was an only child, and Mom and I were close—actually we were best friends. Dad and I were not. Dad was calling to say that we should come to New Jersey in a few weeks, around the beginning of November, to visit them. The fact that he called was alarming in its extraordinariness. I immediately felt my internal systems go on high alert. I wanted to ask, "Is she dying?" but I didn't know how. Instead, I stutteringly asked if anything new had happened. "No," he replied. "Nothing. I just think you should come." He was vague. No more information was forthcoming. Maybe he didn't even know what compelled him to call and request our presence.

I have often wondered about this in the years since these events. I had a sudden flash of the little girl inside of me, my inner child, huddled in the corner of her remembered childhood bedroom in utter confusion, feeling as though her world were falling apart.

For the last year, I had had this knowing, this feeling that the end for my mom was near. This knowing lived somewhere in my gut, but I didn't give it space to be. I ignored it. Pushed it down. Tried not to acknowledge it. Pretended like it wasn't there.

When I got this unusual call from my dad requesting this visit, that knowing part of me stepped forward. That part of me wasn't surprised. It was sad and heartbroken, but not surprised. Chemotherapy was no longer working to keep my mother's pancreatic cancer in check, as it had for the preceding nine years. The doctors and my parents were trying experimental treatments. I was not kept in the loop about much of this. At the time, I didn't realize how much they hadn't kept me in the loop. Perhaps they were protecting me. I don't know. I do know that it hurt to be in the dark, to be invisible. I also know it was a familiar feeling as a woman and a member of this particular family.

Death was not talked about, certainly not with me and not between them, I don't think. I remained alarmed after the call from my dad, the beginning of the untethering of everything I thought I knew. I went to talk to my husband about the possible trip to NJ. I remember also having a therapy appointment on the same day. Coming from a transpersonal, spiritual background, it was important for me to have a therapist that is also holistic, taking spirituality, energy, mind, body, and emotions into account, a therapist that offered something deeper than just talk therapy. This is the type of therapist I am, so I sought the same as part of my support team. I shared the conversation I had with my dad with my therapist, and her intuition told her that we needed to visit my parents sooner than the first week in November, more like the end of October. To me, listening to intuition is a direct connection to Spirit, to my spirit guides working on my behalf. Sometimes, my head is too loud and grounded in the physical realm around me to hear my guides. In this case, someone around me must hear them and relay their messages to me. This was one of those times. The fear inside me was too great to tap into the collective consciousness. My inner child remained huddled and too scared to connect with spirit or anyone.

The combination of my dad's call and my therapist's intuition moved me to action. My husband and I flew from our home in Florida to New Jersey on Thursday, October 26. We planned to stay from Thursday through Sunday. As far as I knew, nothing was happening with my mother. All was status quo, yet my husband and I packed funeral clothes. Why? Intuition said to. Hearing and honoring my intuitive knowing were newfound skills. Throughout my life, I was not taught to honor myself. I was not taught to reside inside myself and listen to my gut or the voice of spirit or intuition. I was taught other focus. I was taught to be a Human Giver, as described by Nagoski and Nagoski. "Human Givers are expected to offer their time, attention, affection, and bodies willingly, placidly, to the other class of people, the 'human beings.'" [7]

In this system, women are the givers. I was raised to give. Being a human giver requires stifling the internal experience, intuition, body knowledge, and spiritual knowledge. I also learned at a young age to act in response to what happened around me rather than

---

[7] DMA Amelia Nagoski and PhD Emily Nagoski, *Burnout: The Secret to Unlocking the Stress Cycle* (Ballantine Books, 2019), p. xiii.

move and act from an internal knowing. Acting in response to and meeting the needs of others was how I learned to be lovable and to get the love I so desperately needed from others. This was one of my greatest survival mechanisms. This is the way that patriarchy trains women to be, trained me to be.

About a week before our scheduled trip on the 26th, my mom went into the hospital. I felt strange being so far away and not knowing what was going on. She could not breathe, and her white blood cell count was too low. I was still told that everything was fine. To me, there is nothing "fine" about going into the hospital.

My husband and I were in the middle of redoing our landscaping. I sent my mom a picture of the finished yard, and she didn't reply. She always replied to me. Always. The lack of response set off my inner alarm bells. They rang through my being, freezing me in place. In hindsight, it was a brief taste of how it would feel when mom was gone and not on the receiving end of texts any longer. I felt lost.

After a day or two, I texted my dad to see if everything was alright with Mom. The response was that she was tired. Everything in me—intuition, felt sense, experience—screamed otherwise. Every part of me screamed that things were not fine. And so, we packed funeral clothes.

This feeling of discordance was familiar to me. I could follow the thread back through time to childhood. This thread of my inner experience not lining up with the experience being presented by those around me as truth. There was a consistent feeling through-out my life in my family of unsteady ground because my reality differed from the reality that my parents inhabited. My experience was repeatedly invalidated, made wrong, or ignored. I learned not to trust my experience. I learned not to trust my intuition. I learned to respond not to what I knew to be true but to what I was told was true so that I could stay loved and lovable. I learned I wasn't enough just by being me, and my experience didn't matter.

This was another of those times when I knew in my gut that something was very wrong and yet was told over and over that everything was fine. Over the course of a lifetime, this way of being left me removed from my felt experience, my body, and my truth. It wove a thread of not-enoughness throughout the tapestry of my being. It moved me through life fragmented, unable to trust my inner knowing, unable to listen to my Self. This feeling of inner distrust was insidious. It slithered through me despite all the personal healing work I had engaged in throughout my life until that point. I had developed powerful survival mechanisms to keep myself safe over the years, and they still sometimes took control over me when perceived trauma, particularly related to the family that I grew up in, was present.

The loss of my mom would be the biggest trauma I could imagine. A deep gutting, impending trauma. My gut said something was very wrong. I was torn between jumping on a plane right then or waiting until our scheduled flight. I slowed things down, reminding myself of all the internal healing work I had done, and I truly checked in with myself. How would I feel if Mom died before I got there? I had the sense that I would be alright. I did not sense that we had any unfinished business. My gut said to wait until our scheduled flight in a few days. We waited, and it was the exact right decision as it placed us with her at the end.

It's so strange how my memory is selective about those few days. Some things are very vivid and live in me like they happened yesterday, while others are vague. For instance, I don't remember the plane ride to NJ, but I remember taking a rideshare from the airport directly to the hospital with all our luggage. It felt weird to enter the hospital with all our luggage. We ran into my cousin in the lobby on his way down from Mom's room. He was visiting from Florida and was now going to the airport. He also seemed to indicate that everything was going to be fine. It was so disconcerting, this feeling like I was alone in the reality I saw around me. Yet, it was familiar, the ground unsettled, chaotic, and ultimately unsafe to be me. This unsteady ground made me hypervigilant, an extra alert, people-pleasing part of me taking over. This part's job was to watch for the danger and discern the way to be loved and stay safe by adhering to the reality of those around me and working to please them rather than the reality I knew inside of me.

When we arrived in my mother's room, my parents greeted us. Mom was attached to oxygen and assorted beeping machines. She seemed happy to see us and asked how long we were staying. This question struck me like a lightning bolt—the answer depended on her death. I knew this. How could I be the only one who knew this? I responded that we were scheduled to leave on Sunday.

We spent the day in the hospital and, in the evening, went with my father back to the house I grew up in, where they still lived. Every time I have visited this house since I moved out as an adult, my mother has had the guest room prepared upon our arrival. This was one of the ways that my mother cared for me.

But this time was different. This time, the couch remained a couch rather than a bed. Searching for the sheets and making the bed was another reminder of the ways that, upon her death, my mother would never care for me again. Soon, I would cease to have a mother in the material realm. This was not something I was ready yet to fully face. It already created chaos and churning inside me even though it wasn't an actual reality yet. I turned away from this knowing and made the bed, moving away from my feelings and felt experience toward the tasks at hand. It's funny how tasks are so much easier than feelings. Our culture repeatedly teaches us to avoid intense feelings and focus instead on business as usual or the tasks at hand. How to separate from our whole Self.

This was largely the way things were in my family, mirroring our larger culture. Grief was a thing to be separate from and continue with business as usual. Emotional experience was also a thing to be separate from and was often dismissed from the familial conversation.

A great example is how my grandmother answered questions about her well-being in later life. Her response is still so vivid to me, though she has been dead since 2004! Even thinking of it now makes my heart ache. When asked how she was, my grandmother usually responded, "No one will listen, so why bother to complain?" She felt that her experience had so little value that she shut it away inside and went on with business as usual, separating her emotional experience from her tasks.

I, in turn, learned that shutting away my emotions and continuing with business as usual was how one got by in life. I realize now that this is how I got by, but it wasn't a way to thrive. This was a cutting off of parts of my Self to be more accepted and lovable. This is another way that patriarchy forces us to fit in the box to be lovable. It makes me wonder, if you don't do the work to unweave patriarchy from your soul, can you thrive?

I was taught to handle grief as separation throughout my life, within my family, and in the larger culture around me. This was a very clear message when my grandfather died. I was still in college, and he died during mid-term exams. This was my first experience watching someone die.

My grandparents had been a part of my life growing up and into adulthood. I spent my summers at their lake house. We were together for all of the holidays throughout the year, celebrating birthdays and anniversaries for the whole family. At the time of my grandfather's death, they lived in our house and were a part of the immediate nuclear family in more ways than just name.

My grandfather died of lung cancer (you'll notice a cancer theme). There were roughly two months between his diagnosis and death. My mom and I cared for him during that time. The night he died, we stayed awake, maintaining a vigil, waiting for him to take his final breath and keeping him as comfortable and loved as possible.

The next morning, I was completely wrung out, like a wet rag. I had one exam that day and called the professor to explain the situation and ask to take the exam on a different day. The response I received was just to come in and take the exam, as though this grief wasn't real or important, as if I was supposed to separate from grief and get back to business as usual. I drove to school and took the exam … business as usual. This was another lesson that there was no space for my grief or my emotional experience. I had to stuff them in a box to meet society's expectations.

When my grandmother died, these cultural and familial messages were reinforced and absorbed by me again. I don't remember my mom having much of a reaction. She cried at the funeral, of course. My mom was the sole caregiver for my grandmother for the seven years between my grandfather's death and my grandmother's. Their lives were intimately, fiercely woven together, and I can't remember my mom ever attending to the loss or grief.

Now, having my own experience of mother loss and the deep gutting that goes with it, I am astonished at what I did not see in my mother at the time. Perhaps she grieved behind closed doors, but based on the family pattern, I think it is more likely that she just went on with business as usual, separating pain and grief from the rest of her. This was the family prescription (and the cultural one). In all ways and all things, we went on with business as usual.

When I consider how my parents handled my mother's illness, I realize that this separation of feelings from the rest of the self, this adherence to business as usual, was their guiding force as I see it. They never acknowledged the possibility of her death, at least to me. They moved through life and battled this illness for nine years without considering end-of-life planning or conversations about it, as far as I could tell. When treatment began to fail, they still did not lean into what was truly present in the here and now, the possibility of death, and what that meant.

Business, as usual, robbed them of present-moment awareness. It robbed them of wholeness and internal healing. As their child, as my mom's best friend, it left me on the outside, feeling invisible and without the knowledge, conversations, and processing that would have helped ease me forward into grief as my mother neared and finally succumbed to death. This kept me separate, feeling less important and unworthy of being in the loop and cared for.

The next day, Friday, we headed back to the hospital. My dad left earlier in his car, and we took Mom's car to have some freedom of movement. When we arrived, Mom was out of bed and sitting in a chair. They were talking about her getting better and coming home. Most of me received this information as a Twilight Zone break from reality. Yet, there was the little girl inside of me who held hope that this might be true, that the way I saw reality was wrong, and she would come home and continue to be Mom. Survival, historically, had often required me to let go of my reality and adhere to the one they existed in. Mom had been battling cancer for so long, and the treatment was taking its toll. The idea that there would be a happy ending did not make sense to the older, wiser me.

The discordance between what I saw as reality and the reality that my parents were living was palpable for me during those last hospital days. It was maddening and left me feeling unsafe, unsettled, confused, and hypervigilant. Here were those familiar childhood feelings once again.

I don't remember much of the rest of that Friday. I know at some point I got Mom's do not resuscitate order (DNR) from the house to give to the doctor. My dad had power of attorney, and as far as I could tell, he didn't believe in DNRs, so I was afraid he would not honor her wishes. Her autonomy over her body and how she was treated seemed vitally important to me. The idea that she could fight so hard for her life and then have her final decisions taken away made me nauseous. There were so many instances of trauma in my past where control over my body was forcefully taken from me, and I was determined not to allow that to happen to my mom in her last moments.

Saturday, when we arrived at the hospital, Mom was in bed and conscious. I don't know what happened during the night, but she was drastically different than the day before. I could see that she was leaving me, leaving the material realm. Her presence was smaller, diminished. She was weak in body and quiet. She could still talk and surprisingly asked my husband how long he thought this would take. We were shocked and stared at her. Suddenly, she inhabited the same reality that we did, and all hope for a happy ending for the little girl inside of me shattered. My husband responded that it would take as long as it takes. She asked for a pastor to be brought in.

That day, she faded in and out of consciousness. I remember talking to the doctor about palliative care and the doctor telling me that they were planning to keep her comfortable using morphine. Having been witness to both my maternal grandmother and grandfather's deaths, I fully understood this to mean that the end was coming, and the medical team would do their best to make it as peaceful as they could.

Peace was certainly what I wanted for my mother. I did not want her to suffer unnecessarily, to struggle to hold onto life when there was no life left. Family visited in a steady stream throughout this day, saying goodbyes. She suffered. She struggled to breathe. She was restless. My father did not allow them to increase the morphine dosage to keep her comfortable, somehow still living in the false reality that she could pull through despite her lungs being ravaged and unable to do their job. I felt tortured watching this play out, watching her struggle and suffer. I sang to her and rubbed her head, as she had done for me throughout my life when I was suffering.

As far back as I can remember when I was in pain, emotional or physical, we would sing songs from *The Sound of Music*, particularly "My Favorite Things." We had the record, and the jacket had a booklet with the lyrics. This was how we dealt with pain. I sang this to her and told her she could move on, that she had done her job with me, and that I would be alright. She hung on and suffered for two more days.

Intuition guided us to sleep in the hospital Monday night. The staff brought us reclining chairs to be a little more comfortable. They brought food and water, hot tea and coffee. I felt cared for in my vigil, my pain, my goodbyes, my complete untethering. It was a reminder that though my mother would be gone, I could and would still receive care if I allowed myself to receive it. She was still hanging on and suffering, though she hadn't been conscious since Saturday afternoon.

On Tuesday morning, we ran home to shower and brush our teeth and returned to the hospital. At around 10:50 am, I watched her breathing get slower and finally stop. I held her hand. Then she was gone. I cried. I broke. I shattered. She was part of the scaffolding that created me. She was part of my essence, my tether.

I moved out of the hospital as if in a dream. I was not in my body. Did I even have a body anymore? It was surreal. The leaves were changing color. It was Halloween. The sun was shining brightly, and yet I was dim. My world had dimmed. Nothing felt real. It was like I was watching a television show. I was completely removed from everything. I was also acutely aware that the world for everyone else moved as if it were any other Tuesday or Halloween, but nothing was the same for me. I was shattered. It was hard to breathe … there wasn't enough oxygen in the air for me. I might as well have been one of the leaves floating on the breeze.

We stopped for pizza on the way home. We needed to eat, and pizza offered me comfort, especially when in NJ. How much easier it was to attend to my body's needs than the needs and pain of my soul. We went to the house that had just lost its heart. The house built by my mother's parents. The house I grew up in. The house that was decorated for Halloween by my mom, just as it had been decorated for every holiday all year long, for the entirety of my life. It has smelled the same forever, and yet, how could it still smell the same when its heart and soul were gone?

I don't remember what came next. I was detached, untethered. Eating, crying, calling the funeral home, going there to make arrangements. My mother ran the household, and my parents had been married for 48 years. She had been in the hospital for more than a week. I worried about outstanding bills. As an only child, it felt like my responsibility to ensure that my dad understood the bills, how to make coffee, and how to do laundry. There were a lot of tasks that needed tending to, which took me away from tending my soul.

I wouldn't quite say that I was avoiding tending to my pain, but I think I needed distance from it in those moments, and there were things that needed to be taken care of. I cried and stayed on task. My husband and I would need to eventually return to our life in Florida, our cats, our jobs, and our house. I also knew that we would need to sell my parent's house, and it would be largely my responsibility to get it ready in person in NJ.

I decided to clean Mom's closet. Looking back, this makes no sense to me other than I was looking for distraction. It felt important at that moment. It was a way to immerse myself in my mother—her chaos, her smells, her Christmas prep. Why did she have so many pairs of slippers? I would dream of this weeks later. She never said goodbye to me at the end, but she would periodically enter my dreams in the coming weeks and talk about things like slippers. As a person deeply engaged in my spirituality, it struck me that she would visit my dreams to talk about slippers. I wanted her to enter my dreams and give me the secrets of the universe … or at least tell me again that she loved and was proud of me.

I found a dress in her closet for the wake. While we had packed clothes for the funeral, I hadn't thought to pack clothes for the wake, and I only had enough clothes for the four days we intended to stay, not the two weeks we actually stayed.

I felt bereft without my mother but oddly not yet alone. The tasks were a friend, or maybe a crutch, supporting and distracting me. My husband was supportive. Friends reached out. My best friend surprised me by arriving with a suitcase of black clothes, some wine, and essential oils to help me sleep and cope (I still use this oil to this day!). Cousins reached out. When people asked, "What do you need?" I answered honestly: food, tights, someone to tell me how to dress.

Historically, I have handled crises myself without asking for or allowing help. This was part of my survival mechanism, not counting on anyone, doing everything myself because I did not trust anyone, and I frequently felt alone throughout my life. As a survival mechanism, it worked to keep me safe. I survived.

This loss changed everything for me. This loss shattered and untethered everything I was. It left me formless smoke. In those moments, the only way to keep myself together was to let those around me in, to receive the help that people offered. I have so many cousins I seldom see, and those that reached out, I let in and let them hold me together, each their own manifestation of Goddess in my life.

We stayed in NJ, getting my dad settled until November 9, when we returned to our cats, our lives, and our jobs. I found I was able to focus on the tasks that needed to be done to set my dad up for some success after the loss of his wife of 48 years despite feeling like I was made of smoke, formless, sad, and shattered.

My parents were from a different time. My mom, despite having a Master's degree in education and being a teacher, took care of the home and most of the Emy-rearing. She never broke out of the box of what society told her she should be, and society told her she should take care of my dad and the house. I think her one rebellion, if you will, was having a career as a teacher, but she still was tasked with caring for the home. After mom's death, we realized pretty quickly that my dad didn't know simple activities of daily living, things like how to do laundry or even make coffee.

It was my first semester of doctoral work. It was already grueling, and I consistently doubted my ability to do this level of work. Consistently doubted my intelligence and fortitude. The thread of not good enough, not enough-ness, woven through my soul was rearing its head as I attempted to navigate grad school.

While we were in NJ, I had fallen behind on schoolwork, something that had never happened in my life previously. I was a classic over-achiever, learning the message early in life that my worth and value were based on my productivity and accomplishments. I was suffering from grief-related brain fog. I had no idea this existed before it hit me like a brick. No one had ever talked to me about what grief does to you.

I was scheduled to return to see my therapy clients the week after our return home. I had no substance, though, no form, no threads holding together the tapestry of my soul. I floated freely in the wind without being able to land, completely unbound. I would sit in front of my computer, and my brain refused to work. When I tried for more than an hour, it resulted in a terrible headache. I was scared. I went from being a smart, capable woman to feeling cognitively impaired ... words wouldn't come to me. I couldn't remember anything at all. It was like the cylinders in my brain just didn't connect. What if I was stuck like this? As someone who had dealt with chronic illness for much of my life, the fear that I wouldn't get my life back was very real for me and based on the reality of the past.

Chapter 2

COMFORT

It was mid-November by the time we got back home and getting close to the holiday season. This has always been my favorite time of year. Typically, it was a time of immense joy that included a lot of decorating and baking. Historically, I decorated for every holiday, as my mom did before me. With so much fog and grief clouding my brain and body, I couldn't do much well, but I could bake and decorate. From the time I was young, my mom and I baked when I was sick or sad. We baked a specific type of chocolate chip cookie. Baking gave me comfort. I leaned into it now when I most needed comfort.

Baking was part of our family's tapestry. It was woven through the fabric of my being like a large blood vessel. It marked holidays, birthdays, sadness, happiness, summers, etc. When my maternal grandmother came to the United States from Germany in the 1930s, she brought recipes and baking traditions that became central to our family culture. There were certain cookies for Christmas, certain breads for New Year's Eve, and certain pies for the summer. And, of course, my mom and I had our special chocolate chip cookie.

Baking offered me solace. Gathering the ingredients and putting them together to create something whole out of individual parts was magical. It was an external representation of what my shattered soul needed on the inside. I was in pieces, smoke-like, and baking was an action that helped me gather the parts into a whole. It was healing. So, I baked. I started with the Emy-feel-better chocolate chip cookies (repeatedly!). As I gathered ingredients and mixed them together, as I tasted dough and dropped it on cookie sheets, I felt my mother with me, looking down at me and standing next to me. It brought me back to a time when I was very young, and I was sick. I was allowed to make the dough for the cookies but not to use the oven until my mom came home from work, and we could do it together. Back then, these cookies made me feel cared for, grounded, and loved. I remember eating the dough as a kid. There were times when very few cookies made it into the oven once my mom got home from work.

One of my prized baking possessions was my copy of the family Christmas recipe book, which my mom's first cousin gifted to me when I married my first husband at age 23.

As the holidays approached, I baked my usual cookies from the family cookbook of German recipes. I also added some of my favorites that Mom used to make and mail to me in Florida. In this way, I kept her with me and found some comfort and easement for myself. It was a way to create wholeness from parts. Though these were cookies I had seen my mom bake every year of my life until I moved to Florida at age 28, I had never made them. I had so many questions that only Mom could answer. Sometimes, I asked her the questions out loud, got really quiet, and tried to hear a response. Mostly, I winged it. While this baking comforted me, it highlighted her absence and the fact that I would never be able to reach out to her for help again. I would be winging it a lot going forward. I was acutely aware of the tension between the comfort I received and the knowledge of her loss. At times, it was like a kick to the gut.

I was in what I now call the acute phase of grief: dysfunctional, seeking comfort in new and old ways. I leaned into baking and my spirituality and spiritual practice, especially my spiritual practice. I spent time connecting with spirit every day. Often, I just lay on the ground crying and asking Goddess to hold me in my grief.

Historically, I handled grief by ignoring it and continuing with business as usual, as the culture around me bade me do. This grief, this cataclysm, was too big even to attempt such a disregard for my feelings. I set the intention to create space for all of my pain, to allow it to be and do what it needed to be and do. This was a challenge since it differed from how I'd traditionally handled grief. This grief was so big and shattering that I did not know how to navigate it. A part of me wanted to control my grief and my feelings about it. This was part of my survival mechanism, turning toward business as usual rather than stopping and feeling my feelings, making friends with them, and giving them space to be how they needed to be. I realized that control was not what would create healing … I needed to surrender to my grief. The healing was in the surrender, not in the control, in the letting it in, not in the ignoring it and pushing it away. The magic was in the turning toward grief and not turning away to business as usual.

Oddly, I had been learning something of surrender in the months preceding Mom's death. Or, maybe not oddly at all. When I look back over the time period directly preceding my mom's death, I feel that for eight months, Goddess had been preparing me for this motherless journey of grief and transformation. My mother on Earth was now gone, but Goddess was always with me. For eight months, I had been learning to lean on Goddess, to surrender to the flow around me, and to receive.

This was still pretty new for me and very contrary to how I had handled trauma and grief in the past, by stuffing it down and going on with business as usual. I realized I needed some support in deepening into surrender. This help and support would come later in the form of local and some not-so-local healers.

The day of my return to sitting in front of clients approached a little more than three weeks after my mom's death. I, however, was made of dust. My brain was mired in fog. I was insubstantial, parts of a whole, like the ingredients of my cookie recipes, but without the way to bake myself back into form (yet). When I considered returning to sit in front of clients, my body tightened and hunched in reaction. Trying to go back to work at that time felt so out of alignment with what I needed. My stomach churned. There was a very strong sense of wrongness about going back to doing therapy. Part of my job as a therapist was to hold the container for my clients, to be the container that holds them as they fall apart, and to help them put themselves back together. At that time, I couldn't even hold myself. I couldn't fathom trying to hold space for anyone else.

Over the years, I had worked hard to be present with my body and listen to it, especially after years of doing the opposite. Thinking was so difficult at this time that the only thing available to me was actual presence, presence with my body, emotions, and heart. In that moment, my body and heart said that I could not sit in front of clients and be caring and effective.

I'm sure this wasn't the first time my body screamed at me for some attention and healing instead of continuing with business as usual.

It may be the first time that I really heard it, though. I canceled the next week of clients and the following week, which was Thanksgiving. The relief was palpable. I felt it in every part of my body and soul. I had created space for my grief and the nothingness of my being in a huge way. I had bucked the cultural system that says that productivity (working) is more valuable than healing.

This was the first time in my life that I created space to fully be exactly how and as I was and to let in all of me. I had a long history of feeling unworthy and not enough, like my needs were not important enough to take up space and time. I was driven throughout my life to prove my lovability—to family, clients, and the world. Part of how I did that was to hustle, to overwork, to produce, to people-please. This is often how women are conditioned to find value in a patriarchal society. Losing my mom shattered and untethered me in such a profound way that it allowed those cultural and transgenerational cages to fall away and dissolve. I was nothing, which was incredibly freeing in many ways and terrifying in others.

My waking hours for those next two weeks were like sleepwalking. Day and night, I was in some in-between state, not knowing what to do, floating from activity to activity. Two things grounded me during that time: baking and my spiritual practice. I continued to lean into them both, taking solace in these two creative forces that were scaffolding me, holding me together in some form. I continued to be present with my body.

My dad came to visit for Thanksgiving. I scheduled clients for the following week. I could again feel the return to work looming, like a thundercloud, knotting my belly. I just couldn't do it. I was not ready. I was still made of smoke, floating uncontained, insubstantial, untethered, like dust in the wind.

A part of me was fearful and anxious, stuck in the belief that to be lovable, valuable, and worthy, I needed to see clients and make money. That fearful, anxious part warred with the part of me that needed to surrender to the process happening around and within me. These two parts have come up again and again: One part stuck in the patriarchal and familial prescription of business as usual, devaluing healing and attending to pain, and another part open to the process of healing, feeling feelings, knowing that worth and value don't come from doing all the things. The part of me that wanted to surrender to the process, that smoke-like part, desperately needed to reorient and attune, to learn who I was, to put the parts back together into a new whole. I realized there is something unique about a loss that untethers and shatters you. From that smoke-like disintegration, you can see all the parts of your tapestry, all the threads that make up your soul, that make you, you.

It allowed me to see that I did not want to fall back into old survival patterns of working hard and over-efforting to be lovable. Instead, I wanted to choose me, my healing, my reweaving, and my needs. Oof, this was a significant departure for me. I was scared. In assessing what I felt I needed at the time, I thought I could take a month off to focus on my healing and return to work after the holidays in the new year. Of course, that part of me that needs to DO something to feel valuable decided that I could use this time to catch up on schoolwork. Even in my decision to surrender, I still couldn't do it completely.

How many times during my life had I chosen ME completely? I couldn't think of one. But this was the beginning of leaning fully into healing instead of business as usual. My brain was still clouded by fog, making mental tasks, including schoolwork, feel like slogging through a tar pit.

I had taken incompletes in all of my classes when mom died as I was incapable of completing tasks that required my brain. This pressed against the part of me that thought my value was found in productivity. Never in my life had I not turned in coursework on time nor taken an incomplete, let alone three! Despite the brain fog and concentration difficulties, I was able to get everything done for school before the deadline in mid-December and shift my focus to baking and being (not doing).

Baking brought me closer to my mom. It was making something whole and delicious out of parts and ingredients. It grounded me. It fed and nourished my soul. It helped me know I still existed. It was a process. I could trust it. Follow these steps with these ingredients, and you will have a specific result, a finished product.

It reminded me to trust the process of my healing, even though there was no recipe to follow, and I didn't know the end result. I was absolutely certain that I would transform into something more. While I didn't know it at the time, when I was actually in the muck and the healing journey, part of my motivation for studying this journey and forming a process and a way to find my way home to my authenticity was to create a map so that you wouldn't have to figure this all out on your own.

This soul-feeding practice of baking also created tension within me. You see, I had struggled with disordered eating and body image issues for much of my life. Here I was, finding a practice, baking, that nourished me, grounded me, scaffolded me, and there was a part inside of me screaming at me about getting fat, which in turn meant that I would lose value.

This may sound ridiculous to those of you who have never struggled with disordered eating, but for me, being thin was one of the things I believed made me valuable, lovable, and desirable (which increased my lovability and value). Over the years, being dedicated to my healing journey, I had attempted to heal my disordered eating in therapy and on my own and managed to shift some aspects of it. The disintegrating nature of Mom's death intersecting with what had become the vital healing scaffolding of baking allowed me to more clearly see the thread of disordered eating woven into the tapestry of my being, woven throughout my soul. I could zoom out and see the patterns and how they connected back to my mom and to the patriarchal system within which I was raised. The thin ideal is one of the ways that patriarchy polices women, keeps us stuck, and keeps our attention diverted from what is really important. It keeps us "less than," always working for the angle to make us valuable, worthy … equal.

I could see how these threads woven through my mom's tapestry contributed to her death and how they contributed to unhealthiness in my life. Once I was attuned to this particular discordant disordered eating thread in my tapestry, I could see its history and where it came from, and I could see that it was never mine to carry. I carried it for my mom. This thread was woven in the tapestry of my energetic being by the scaffolding created by my mom that helped shape me. When she died, that scaffolding crumbled. And from my untethered, floating, liminal space, I could see.

What I saw shocked me: pieces of a very large puzzle clicking together like dominoes in my head. While my mom was in the hospital dying, my uncle, her brother, kept talking about calling her "Fatty" as her nickname growing up. As a daughter, hearing this broke my heart. As a therapist, hearing this added pieces to the puzzle of me and my relationship with food and my body.

Later, from my zoomed-out position, I remembered this and could trace the thread of my disordered eating to my mother's past. I also remember hearing the doctor say that Mom was malnourished when she came into the hospital. I assumed that this was because of her cancer treatment, but when we arrived at my parent's house during her hospital stay, the refrigerator held skim milk. I felt furious seeing that. For months, the doctors had been telling her that she needed to gain weight to avoid having a feeding tube, yet here, the fridge was stocked with fat-free milk! I understand very well the pull of the disordered eating gremlin inside my head, but to think that that gremlin had such a strong pull on my mom that she couldn't see to her well-being during a time when her life was threatened blew my mind completely.

This was highlighted for me about six months before Mom died. She was visiting me in Florida. She was deep into treatment for her pancreatic cancer, and she was rail thin. I was trying to convince her to come out and get some french fries and a milkshake to help her gain weight. She responded that she didn't want to gain too much weight. This was my first clue about her disordered eating. I don't know why I never saw it. I knew my history and struggles, but I didn't see the depth of her struggle until that moment. She was dying, yet the grip of being a certain size, maintaining her lovability and value, and shedding the nickname Fatty held firm and didn't allow her to care for herself. Our culture taught her that her value as a woman was based on her body size, and this outweighed her very survival.

The final piece of the disordered eating puzzle came about six months after Mom died. I was attending a peer group meeting with a few other therapists. One of the other therapists mentioned that premature babies have a higher percentage of eating disorders. My mom was born prematurely and was force-fed every two hours for the beginning of her life, never learning her body's signals for hunger and satiety. When I heard about this connection, I had an immediate physical reaction. I started to sweat. My vision blurred and narrowed. My breath became shallow. All of the disordered eating puzzle pieces came together at once, producing a physical trauma reaction within me. It was handy at that moment to be in a room full of therapists who could help me ground and talk me through this new knowledge as it settled within me.

I wasn't able to see much of this until after Mom's death. The untethering, shattering nature of the loss opened the healing portal, allowing me to see more. During this time, I couldn't think well, but I floated in liminal space, following my internal experience and my internal knowing.

By beginning to allow my grief space to be, I entered the healing portal. I could clearly see this thread of disordered eating, could see that it was woven into my being by Mom, could see it attaching me to her and leading away. I sat in spiritual practice and asked spirit about this thread, "Is this mine to carry? Is this important to me? Does thinness define me?" I tuned into the answer from deep within and from Goddess around me, and what I heard whispered deep in my soul was no. No, this is not mine to carry. No, thinness does not define me or define my value. No, I did not need to keep this thread as part of my tapestry. It would take a bit longer until I fully understood that I needed to release it actively. For now, I attuned to and understood it, me, my mom, and our history considerably more.

The holidays passed with much baking and its accompanying healing. I actively tried to send love and compassion to the part of me
that was very anxious about gaining weight. In so many ways, the
holidays were joyless that year. Baking helped me stay close to Mom
and helped me trust my process. I began to explore ways to heal my
disordered eating thread, such as intuitive eating, not quite understanding that what was actually needed was the spiritual release of
the thread.

Intuitive eating as a concept made sense to me. I had long felt that
there must be a way to arrive at an ideal weight that didn't involve
being on a perpetual diet (the way the culture around me insisted
I should be). A way that my body could be how it needed to be. I
had already been learning to tune in to my intuition more, which
seemed a natural addition to that practice.

Reading about intuitive eating and beginning to eat intuitively created an abundance of space and allowance within me. Intuitively, I
was called to bake and consume things from my childhood as part
of my healing process. Once I allowed this as a practice, the tension
between the anxious part of me that needed to remain thin to be
lovable and the part that needed the solace offered by baking dis-
solved, and I could take care of myself and my healing needs. These
preliminary acts of healing and permission paved the way for me
to fully release this thread from my tapestry in the coming months.

In January, it was time to resume working with my psychotherapy
clients. I still wasn't ready. Here again was the tension between following my socially created and trauma-created need to be valuable
by working, to be valuable and lovable to my husband, my clients,
and society in general, on the one hand, and the intuitive knowing
that I was not ready and needed to continue on my healing journey.

I succumbed to the cultural requisite to return to work, to be valuable and lovable by doing and producing. I denied my needs and ignored my intuition, as I had so often throughout my life, as I had been taught. I returned to business as usual. I was still made of smoke and fragmented, like a broken mirror on the ground. Brain fog was ever present, stealing my words and stopping my thoughts from forming and connecting when they did form. Each day, I dreaded going into my office. I had very little of myself to give, yet I was pulled by the cultural idea that I should be working. These were the messages I received from everyone around me throughout my entire life. My soul screamed for healing. My soul screamed for me to stop working and give myself completely to my healing process. My dreams affirmed this. Goddess whispered this in my ear during each daily meditation.

I woke one day in February, and I just knew. I knew I couldn't continue the way I was. It felt vital to take a few months off and shift my full attention to healing. It was an imperative. I must allow space for my full untethering, relinquishing and releasing bonds, threads, and stories from the past and reclaiming things lost. I must lean into my smokiness and allow the threads of my being to settle so I could reweave them into their new, fully Emy tapestry. To continue with business as usual would keep me forever fragmented, inauthentic, and lacking wholeness.

I realized that until this point in my grief and healing journey, I wasn't able to fully rest into healing because I always felt the pressure of an end date, a back-to-work date, a date after which my focus would be on others and not myself. This end date prevented me from fully leaning into my dissolution, like a caterpillar in a cocoon. While I was able to begin the healing process around some of my mom's threads woven into my energetic body, such as disordered eating, I was not fully committed to the healing journey, and that hampered me.

During those months of tension between the cultural prescription to work and the internal need to turn toward my healing, I was only half committed to my healing journey. One foot remained in the business-as-usual paradigm of separation, where the needs and desires of others, including society at large, were placed before my own needs, desires, authenticity, and wholeness.

Business as usual valued money and success over personal healing. Business as usual thought I could separate the shattered part of me from the rest of me and keep going, keep seeing clients, keep doing. But this was an untethering loss. All parts of me were dust, and there was no way to separate the grieving parts from the whole. Doing that would have been abandoning my soul and betraying my Self, something that I have done in the past that has led to anxiety and physical illness.

For those couple of months following Mom's death, I clung to the idea that I could recover and be fine in a few weeks, maybe six, and carry on. I was still attached to the idea of a speedy return to "normal." I didn't yet understand that there would be no return to the old me—only a reorientation, reorganization, releasing, reclaiming into someone entirely new, entirely ME.

Working with healers in the physical realm and my spirit guides in the imaginal realm allowed me to decide to fully lean into my healing journey. This was a commitment to releasing the threads that were part of the old ways of being, the old patterns and fears. It was a commitment to Self, healing, creating the path by walking, rewriting, reclaiming, and reweaving me. A commitment to being vulnerable and uncertain and trusting the process, Goddess, and myself. To choose to fully lean into grief and transformative healing was unheard of in my life up to this time, yet I knew that I must take a considerable period away from my psychotherapy practice, away from the concerns of others, to focus on my own.

In a world that requires women specifically to be other focused, this was revolutionary. For someone with my upbringing, feeling less than and like I needed to prove my worth and lovability by doing and producing, this was an outright insurrection. But I knew this was the only way to fully honor myself and my healing journey. I did not know who I was in the world anymore. How could I sit in front of clients half-formed, unaware, and smoke-like and help them with their journey to authenticity? It was impossible.

Making this decision to lean into my healing journey created an incredible amount of tension between the part of me that knew I needed to dedicate time to my healing and the part of me that had always felt not good enough, the part that over-efforted to prove my worth and value.

This latter part became agitated at the prospect of losing all my clients, of never getting any more clients, and ultimately of being valueless, unlovable, and unloved by everyone and everything, including my husband and myself. This feeling of fear around my business wasn't new. It was part of my anxiety of always feeling on the cusp of people realizing I wasn't worthy, of doing the wrong thing, and being abandoned as unlovable. It took a lot to turn toward the pain and step into the healing portal when everything and everyone around me was telling me to go back to business as usual, to get over it, to stuff it down, and to ignore it. It's brave as fuck to stop, feel, and walk toward healing. And it was terrifying.

I was now in direct opposition to the cultural and familial chains that said that taking care of myself was selfish and not a valid use of time. Value came from other care and doing/producing. By deciding to lean into healing, I chose myself in a way I never had before.

During my life, I betrayed my inner truth countless times in service to getting love, being lovable, and feeling worthy. At times, my body responded with chronic illness. Choosing myself this time was possibly the most healing corrective experience of my life to that point. It was the catalyst that allowed all the healing that came afterward. It was as though my healing was stuck behind a dam.

Making this decision released the flow of healing, and I began reforming myself into the wholeness tapestry, reclaiming my missing soul parts, healing, and releasing threads that were not mine to carry. I was moving toward freedom. My body began to shed layers of intense cultural chains that were keeping me stuck, keeping me less than. I was free to be in my process, to rest if my body needed rest, to bake, clean, cook, read, and binge Netflix. Wherever my process, intuition, and Goddess led me, I followed. It was liberating and empowering. My spirit was unencumbered, even though this journey was painful. I rested into the flow around me and let go into nothingness, allowing Goddess to hold, form, and move me.

In so many ways, it might have been easier to stay with business as usual, easier to keep living from old patterns of survival born from trauma, and easier to care for others rather than myself. I had always done it this way. Living from survival had worked throughout my life, right? I had survived, but I wasn't all that I could be. I wasn't living a fully expressed, authentic whole life. Maybe if I

hadn't made the monumental decision to step fully into my healing journey, my wounds would have healed over as they had in the
past, but they would have impacted my life in the form of anxiety,
depression, dissatisfaction, and physical illness, as they had so many
times before, like the scar tissue that forms around a foreign object
lodged in flesh and not removable. Staying as I was may have
appeared easier on the surface, but it would have kept me from
health, wholeness, and true healing. It would have perpetuated a
cycle that kept me small and sick and prevented me from access-
ing my full power and energy.

Having made this incredible decision to honor myself and my healing journey, I focused on the logistics that would make it possible
to stop work for many months. At the time, I believed it would be
only three or four months, but having learned my lesson about end
dates keeping me from being fully immersed in my healing, I didn't
actually decide on an end date for this journey. I was determined
to follow my intuition, my process, and my spirit. I realized that I
needed to ask my father to borrow money from my inheritance
of my mother's estate. I needed to discuss things with my husband.
The prospect of these two conversations filled me with trepida-
tion. For that thread within my soul's tapestry that believed that my
worth and value came from doing/producing, this was tantamount
to saying I was a loser. I was showing up and saying that I was going
to stop producing. It was like saying I was a failure and had no
value any longer. It was so hard to have those conversations! And
I pushed through the fear. I leaned into that other thread, the one
that was just awakening and becoming vibrant and alive, the one
that whispered, "Yesssssss. Do this for you. Become all of yourself,
fully realized, whole, healed, YOU."

My husband expressed the valid concern that I would get stuck in grief and never go back to work. I say this is a valid concern because there was a part (only a part) of me that shared that same fear. A much larger part of me could already feel the changes happening inside me solely because I decided to lean into grief and transformational healing. I could feel that inside of me, there were no stuck parts. I was so ready for true transformational healing, the kind that can only happen when you decide to walk through the healing portal and embark on the transformational work of releasing, reclaiming, and anchoring in wholeness.

Logistically, I needed to attend to my clients. It was important to do my best for them to feel cared for and not abandoned in my absence. I referred them to other therapists. For those clients who were appropriate for monthly sessions, I decided to come into the office one three-day week per month. This kept my skills honed and brought in enough money to pay the office rent.

Having worked out the fiscal, vocational, and relational parameters of this sabbatical, I turned my attention to the healing itself. Big transformational healing requires guides, both in this Earthly realm and in the spiritual/imaginal realm. I knew that I needed healers to help scaffold my healing work. I also knew that my spirituality and spirit guides would play a significant role in the work ahead. These two different types of guides would hold a frame for me to function within since the scaffolding I lived within for my lifetime crumbled away with my mom's death. My most important guide during this healing time was Goddess herself, the Great Mother. Though I had eight months of awakening to Goddess before Mom's death, I realized that Goddess had been present in my life even before those eight months, and my engagement with her at this critical time was a resurgence rather than a new relationship.

She was present in the books I read as a child, like *The Mists of Avalon* and *Women Who Run With the Wolves*. She was present in the belligerent second-wave feminism that possessed and guided me through my late teens and early twenties. While I did not consciously recognize her workings as Goddess, looking back, I believe I knew her, and she knew me. Even with Goddess working in my life from an early age, I still fell victim to the bindings of patriarchy that created me and viewed my value only in relation to men and production and not my own beingness.

Chapter 3

GUIDES ALONG THE WAY

The reawakening of Goddess in my life prior to Mom's death began simply enough with a search on Pinterest for Goddess tattoo ideas. I can't remember what propelled me to begin this search. Perhaps She was calling, and my mind was quiet enough at that moment to hear Her. It was a bit out of character for me to search for random Goddess tattoo ideas. I have multiple tattoos; each was chosen and created because of an important event, feeling, or healing in my life. None were chosen because I liked a picture at random. They all had deep meaning to me and my life. This simple search for Goddess tattoos led me down a rabbit hole of reading about the Goddesses in the pictures I found. Their stories and pictures stirred something in my soul—recognition, awareness, longing. They quickened my pulse and made me feel alive and of value because I was me, a woman.

I was raised Christian and never saw myself reflected in the God I was taught. I never felt valued as a woman, as a human being. I felt less than, not enough. Seeing the Divine with a female face offered me the ability to see myself in the Divine, to know that there was value in being female, that I had value. I felt empowered.

What started as an innocent search for pictures became much deeper and more important. It began to lay the framework for all the healing that would come. I felt Goddess calling me, pulling me, and my answering longing for Her embrace and support, but I had no idea where or how to go deeper than random searches on Pinterest or Google. I reached out to a friend who I knew had a deeper spiritual connection and practice than I did, and she pointed me to the work of Chameli Ardagh and the Awakening Women Institute (AWI).

Discovering AWI felt like coming home to a place where I belonged, felt valued, and loved by Goddess just for being me. Chameli Ardagh and the work of AWI were my guides to creating a deep embodied relationship with Goddess and myself.

Before this time, I would have described myself as spiritual but not someone with a living, vibrant relationship with the Divine. Engaging in sadhanas (spiritual practice) with AWI helped me create a living relationship with Spirit that is sustainable and sustaining. I hadn't previously known or understood the importance of this in my life.

I discovered that this connected relationship with Goddess was a missing piece of my healing picture. I was raised under the modern American standard of medical care that separates the body from the mind and spirit. Though I was trained as a holistic psychotherapist, when I was previously headed toward burnout in my therapy practice, I only addressed my physical symptoms. The cultural tapestry of separation was woven around me and through me, encouraging me to only address physical symptoms or mental health symptoms. By adding a connection to Goddess, I felt a shift toward a more whole, entwined view of everything: health, Self, and my work in the world. This relationship with spirit awakened, enlivened, and energized me and started me on the path to transformational healing and wholeness.

Chameli Ardagh and AWI were the first guides on my journey, and they, in turn, led me to my spirit guides, different faces and aspects of Goddess. At the beginning was Lalita Devi. "The Goddess Lalita Devi is a much-needed archetype of the spiritually and erotically awake feminine. She points us to a source of wisdom and empowerment which is found through embodied intimacy with ourselves and the world."[8] My first 21-day sadhana (spiritual practice) focused on Lalita Devi. Daily emails arrived with spiritual practices for 21 days, plus three two-hour live retreat calls during the 21 days. This was my portal into spiritual embodiment.

I was initially drawn to Lalita Devi because of her focus on the erotic embodied feminine. For much of my early life, my engagement with my sexuality was a means to an end, a perceived way for me to be lovable or get the love I needed (in reality, this left me lonelier than I could have realized because I was disconnected from my self and misaligned from my inner truth). I was drawn to the idea of the erotic embodied feminine because it was powerful. It was owning my sexuality and eroticism not as a means to an end but for pleasure and joy. Lalita Devi helped me to come home to this.

I would participate in two more sadhanas with different Goddesses, Durga and Sarasvati, before my mom died, giving me a pretty solid foundation to rest on upon her death when I shattered into dust.

---

[8] "Lalita Devi: The Healing Power of the Erotically Awake Feminine," Awakening Women Institute, November 18, 2023, https://awakeningwomen.com/shop/21-day-lalita-devi-sadhana/.

These two particular Goddess sadhanas contributed greatly to my healing journey despite happening before my mom died.

"Durga is a warrior Goddess, mirroring to us genuine feminine empowerment. In the Hindu mythology, where the story of Durga has its origin, the demons that she is fighting represent the forces and compulsive patterns which freeze us, which generate conflict, separation, and delusion. The gods and goddesses mirror to us clarity, love, compassion, and awakened consciousness."[9] Mom's death separated all the parts of my Self, allowing me to see threads of patterns and forces not my own. Durga was one of my spirit guides, gently nudging me to see what was in front of and around me. She was another part of the scaffolding that allowed me to walk the path of reweaving my soul into wholeness. She helped me to stand in my power, to make decisions for my well-being, to be revolutionary, and to break the chains of business as usual. She was a warrior and taught me to be one as well. She stood by my side and walked through the fire with me.

Sarasvati is a Goddess of creative expression, the arts, wisdom, and sound. The sadhana with Sarasvati was the catalyst for my return to graduate school for my Ph.D. at a time when going back to school and earning my doctorate was the furthest thing from my mind. She guided me back to school to deepen my knowledge of spiritual and soul-based healing, whispering to me about my mission and path in the world, urging me forward on my healing path so that I could then help others in a different way.

---

[9] "Durga: Rooted in the Authority of Love," Awakening Women Institute, November 18, 2023, https://awakeningwomen.com/shop/21-day-durga-sadhana/.

After Mom's death, but before I made the concrete decision to give myself fully to my healing and transformative process of reweaving my soul, I began to gather around me healers in the material realm who would become some of my guides as I journeyed. It was important that these healers in the material realm felt like good connections for me in my body and soul. I needed their energy to resonate with my energy, and I wanted to be able to feel their relationship with the Divine. I worked hard to stay deeply connected to my internal landscape as I interacted with potential guides on my journey. I needed these people to hold a safe container for me and to help me move more deeply into my healing journey.

One of these guides was my therapist, an energy healer; one was a Priestess of Avalon, Ashley Smith; and the third was a Medicine Woman, Shinai Schindler. I had been following Ashley and Shinai on Facebook for months and had been working with my therapist for a few months. Shinai was an intuitive energy healer and conducted spiritual energetic healing in her office, which was set up like a therapy office but with more crystals and burning sage (right up my alley!). Ashley conducted rituals and sacred tea ceremonies for women at the new and full moons, and energetic, spiritual, one-on-one healing sessions.

Sacred tea ceremonies called to me, partly because they were called Awakening Woman Tea Ceremonies, though not affiliated with AWI. Awakening felt like at least a part of what was happening for me, at least before Mom's death. My first attendance at a sacred tea ceremony was a few months before Mom died. I was nervous about attending, the thread of not-enoughness running through my tapestry creating a story about being found wanting in any new situation, lacking worth and value. My intuition pulled me, and Goddess called me forward, beckoning me to begin creating the scaffolding that would hold me in the coming months. Despite my nervousness, going to the sacred tea ceremony felt right. I could feel this rightness in my gut and my bones. It was different than anything I had experienced before, with AWI sadhanas and retreats happening completely online. This was an in-person women's circle. I had a long history of feeling like I didn't belong at home, in school, everywhere. What if I experienced that in a women's circle? Where would I ever belong? Feel valuable? Enough?

The ceremony took place in a transformed church. Upon my arrival, I saw candles burning throughout the church and other women milling about. The energy was reverent, peaceful, and safe. The belonging I felt in the online AWI community was mirrored here in this in-person women's circle. I realized that this is Goddess energy, the way She welcomes and loves Her priestesses. Over my life, I hadn't often experienced feeling safe, held, accepted, valued, as if I belonged. I did here, with this group of women, reveling in Goddess energy. This feeling of belonging, being held and loved for being me, began to restore and heal a piece of my soul that long ago learned that I wasn't enough just as I was and would never belong because of who I was. This part never felt good enough and worked hard at over-efforting and DOING to be valuable. Goddess does not require this. Goddess loved me as I was, and I felt that in my body and soul.

A sacred tea ceremony is conducted without talking. Dancing and exclaiming are encouraged and welcomed. The tea, the music, and the ceremony are designed to induce an altered state of consciousness. I could feel the intentional energy flowing through the church, surrounding us, weaving us together, even before Ashley began the ceremony formally. Ashley's movements as she poured and served the tea were intentional and ritualistic. The repetition lulled me. I watched her hands, heard the drumming pumping through the speaker, and felt my consciousness expand. I felt Goddess in the room, in my soul, in my heart, in my energy field. I drank tea and floated in Goddess' embrace. It was an awakening, a homecoming to me, a preparation. I was fully present in body and soul. It was juicy, alive, potent.

This was the only time I participated in a tea ceremony before Mom's death, but in that liminal space after her death, during that first holiday period when I was trying to understand how to heal and what I needed, my soul knew that Ashley would be one of the guides on this healing journey.

I reached out to her and called her in as a healer almost as soon as we returned from NJ after Mom died. I felt similarly about Shinai and began working with her in November 2017. Once the decision was made in February to fully lean into my transformational journey of healing and wholeness, I made a more consistent schedule of meeting with and working with Ashley and Shinai every other week. As I moved through the healing process, I would add other guides, particularly related to the body. As was typical of me and my compartmentalizing, I left the body out of my healing ventures at the beginning, just like for years, I left spirit and soul out of my attempts to heal my body. Wholeness was coming, though.

Chapter 4

HEALING

Those first few months of tension, from October 31, 2017, when Mom died, through February 2018, when I decided to fully commit to my healing journey of reweaving the tapestry of my soul, set the stage for the rest of my healing journey. While some profound healing happened during that liminal time, the most important aspect of that time was my attuning to the healing matrix that would carry me for the rest of the journey.

For months, I sat in the tension between what I needed for healing (a break from work, baking, resting into my grief, resting into Goddess) and what culture, family upbringing, and past trauma dictated I should do (ignore feelings, prove my worth and value by working, prove my worth and value by being thin, over-efforting).

In the end, standing at the crossroads of the healing portal and business as usual, I chose me and healing and wholeness. I chose to lean into grief and healing, and this decision, this resting into my truth, was stepping into the portal of healing, attuning to the healing matrix that would surround me for the duration of this journey.

During the healing period, I began attending to the part of me that was eating disordered throughout my adulthood and began to work with the part of me that has always felt not good enough, the part that thought she had to over-effort to prove her worth and value. I released and unwove those threads that didn't serve me and weren't mine to carry and reclaimed those threads and parts that had been cut off due to trauma and learning repeatedly that it wasn't alright to be me, that I wasn't alright. The river of healing was undammed. The journey took 10 months of intense work until I came to a place where I could do the work of anchoring it all into wholeness, feeling substantive, connected, and complete once more, but actually more than I ever was.

Different Types of Healing

Deciding to enter the healing portal was a huge step on the journey home to my true essence. I engaged with various modalities of healing once I made this decision. In truth, however, once I entered the healing portal, it was like being meditative at all times. While I did specific things for healing, like biweekly sacred tea ceremonies with Ashley, sometimes I would have profound insights when doing everyday things like washing dishes. The healing matrix moved, created, and worked me at all times of the day and night once I opened to it and healing.

"Journeying" was one of my primary healing modalities and a large part of the healing matrix itself. I define "journeying" as traveling in and through the spirit realm, as opposed to the material realm where I, and most people, generally exist daily. It is a meditative state and a trance state—a voyage into the realm beyond what your eyes see, deep into the psyche, where spirit guides and insights live. I can journey easily when in a meditative state or engaged in my spiritual practice. This is the realm where I can speak directly to Goddess, where I can see her and be with her. This is the realm where much of my healing occurred. Through journeying, I could release those threads that didn't serve me and reclaim my lost soul parts.

Since I began working with Goddess and deepening into spiritual practice and meditation, I have been adept at dropping into an altered state of consciousness. This altered state allows me to be close to Goddess, allows me to journey, and facilitates my releasing of parts of my soul's tapestry that don't serve me and the reclaiming of those soul parts that were lost. While my ability to access this altered state was always available to me, within the healing matrix, I existed so close to this space that dropping in became as easy as the blink of an eye.

I regularly met with Ashley and Shinai for one-on-one healing sessions. Work with Ashley always involved a tea ceremony, another of the healing modalities in the healing matrix, followed by spiritual healing based on what she was given to know by spirit during the journeying we did.

Work with Shinai didn't involve tea ceremony but was instead energetic healing, ritual, ceremony, and, of course, journeying. I also regularly participated in Ashley's Awakening Woman Tea Ceremonies at the full and new moon, journeying regularly with a circle of women. Daily, I engaged in meditation and spiritual practice, and these were the foundational cornerstones of my healing journey. They kept the healing energy flowing through the matrix.

Historically, regarding healing, I had an unhelpful habit of not attending to all of the parts of my Self. Though I thought of myself as holistic, there were times I only focused on my body, or only focused on my spirit, or only focused on my emotional health. Doing things this way often kept healing from being overwhelming but never allowed for complete healing.

One day in October of 2018 (fully a year after Mom died!), I woke up knowing I was neglecting my body within the healing matrix. Until this point, I was focused entirely inward, on my soul, my spirit, and the spiritual realm. I awoke knowing I needed to add something to my practices that included the body or was focused on the body alone.

My body felt unintegrated. My right foot and knee hurt for no discernible reason. I was on some strange illness cycle where I felt like I was getting sick, was sick, and was getting over being sick every two weeks, over and over again. I had been so focused on my emotional and spiritual pain that I hadn't noticed what else was happening in my body. I needed someone who could integrate the structure of my body. Did something like that even exist? It turned out that it did, and it was even called structural integration! I got a referral from my therapist for someone who did this type of work. Structural integration works the body's fascia to help every part of the body align and function better. It is painful and also feels deliciously good. It's based on the work of Ida Rolf and works with the body as a whole over multiple sessions to align all parts of the mechanical body. I hated it because it was somewhat painful, and I loved it because it drastically changed how my body felt and moved through the world. It was another external representation of all of the reorganization that was happening inside of my soul.

Once I got started with structural integration, offering my body some healing and relief from pain, I wondered what took so long. How did I miss something so critical to whole person healing? But I knew the answer. This was business as usual. Separating parts of the self. This was how I was raised. The body was a thing to be fixed with medicine and the like and was separate from the mind, emotions, soul, and spirit. It occurred to me that my realization to bring the body into my healing was a profound piece of healing for me in and of itself. There was a reclaiming of the body as part of the whole. Adding this physical healing work felt like finding a missing piece to the healing matrix. Structurally integrating my body felt like it helped all of the other healing integrate more fully into my soul.

Another adjunctive aspect of my healing involved participating in professional and personal trainings related to my healing journey. I followed where my intuition led in this domain and attended a training for leading women's temple, a training on energy psychology, and participated in an empath mastery online course.

I was already deepening my relationship with my feminine Goddess-based spirituality. Learning how to serve other women with similar longings fed my soul. Much of my healing involved my energetic body, so training in comprehensive energy psychology also deepened my healing and added depth to my work as a therapist. Finally, I have always identified as an empath and highly sensitive person. Participating in an online course on harnessing those traits while guarding myself from burnout was vitally important to my personal healing and work as a therapist.

I continued to engage with my doctoral work as well, though I did it in a way that was different from how I had previously. I started to write myself back into being. Much, if not all, of my schoolwork focused on or around the healing work that I was so actively living. This focus deepened the healing work as the healing work deepened my schoolwork in turn. I felt a bit like a child in a candy store, unfettered by society's and my own rules about productivity and focus on Self. I followed where the call led me.

I decided to walk through the healing portal at the end of February 2018. The logistics took about a month to get organized. As I mentioned previously, it was essential to me that my clients felt cared for as I referred them to appropriate therapists to continue their work. During the month of logistical preparation, I worked bi-weekly with Shinai and Ashley, engaging with the healing matrix around me. My grief was interwoven with the healing matrix, and both flowed around me and through me like two threads dancing on a windy day.

How Can I Have a Birthday but Not a Mother?

Mom and I shared a birthday month, March, and as that first day of the month rolled around, I was plagued by the question, "How can I have a birthday but not have a mother?" The untethered feeling that had been with me since Mom died felt even more pronounced in the days that led up to our birthdays. They were three days apart, far enough that I didn't feel cheated out of my special day as a child and close enough that it always felt like sharing a special bond with her. And now, here I was, missing the other half of the special birthday bond. I felt a deep emptiness in my heart and soul, a special kind of loneliness that I later termed "existential aloneness."

This was my first birthday since her death. My first birthday without a mother in the world. Mom's birthday was the 17th, and mine was the 20th. I realized that I wanted, maybe needed, to honor both in a big way and in a different way than ever before.

Everything felt surreal. How could I continue to exist in the world without a mother? I had a birthday, but no mom. It was jarring, discordant, like music notes completely out of tune with the rest of the song. I felt wrong.

At the same time, I longed to create something special, to attend to these momentous days in a retreat space, to mark them in a healing way. I spoke with Ashley about creating a one-on-one bespoke retreat, and while this wasn't her usual practice, she agreed to work with me and plan something. As with all things during this time, I was creating the path by walking and following where intuition and Goddess led me.

Mom's birthday was on a Saturday. I planned to meet Ashley at the retreat center that afternoon and be in a ritual, healing space for almost two full days. The weekend would include a sacred tea ceremony, labyrinth walking, fire dancing, and a womb-cleansing ritual.

The healing work that I was doing was bigger and deeper than my mom's death. Her death shattered me in a way that allowed me to see the full tapestry of my soul and attune to the discordant, unhealed threads from my past. Some of these threads were related to my history of sexual assault, some were connected to growing up bound by the chains of patriarchy, some were related to my relationship with food and my body, and some were related to the roles I played in my family growing up, the messages I internalized about who I was and how I got the love that I desperately needed.

Once I decided to walk through the healing portal into the healing matrix, the dam of healing was breached. So much of this work stemmed from the initial decision to engage in this journey. I sifted through the threads that made up the tapestry of my soul—healing those parts that needed it, releasing those parts that were never mine to carry, reclaiming those cutoff threads, and healing them into a harmonious vibration with the rest of my soul.

Birthday Retreat

I expected the retreat to be magical. Expected that two full days of being in deep connection with Goddess and doing ritual, embodied, spiritual work would shift and heal large parts inside of me. This was another lesson in being with what is actually happening, resting into the now rather than having expectations.

The day I was to leave for the retreat was Mom's birthday. I packed my things and was present with my internal landscape. I had already begun to shift into the spirit realm, the place of ceremony, ritual, Goddess. I was only half present with the material realm where my body existed as I packed for the weekend. Then I got a text from my husband saying that his young adult daughter wanted to move in with us as she found her way in life after finishing college the year before.

At any other time, this would have been an easy yes with appropriate boundaries. But being asked this question of adding another person to our household at that moment, in the throes of grief, already vulnerable and very present with the loss of my mother, I felt like I didn't matter, like my pain was irrelevant, my healing irrelevant. My loss, pain, and healing process went unrecognized by anyone but me. The question of whether she could move in with us wasn't one I felt safe answering honestly. I felt stuck again between what society said I should do, which was say yes, of course, and what I needed to do: care for myself, attend to my grief and healing, and maybe say no, or at the very least have my pain acknowledged and figured into the decision process.

The pain for me wasn't around the yes or no answer but in the experience of feeling as though my grief and healing process were irrelevant (which translated into my old narrative of being irrelevant). In their irrelevance to those around me, they were also expected to be irrelevant to me. I felt a shift in that moment, the shift from people around me being supportive to feeling like I should be over it and get on with business as usual. Yet, for me, it was nowhere near over and done.

My sabbatical from work was about to start in a week. This mini-retreat was the great kick-off to my full commitment to my healing journey. Instead of being able to rest into that healing journey, my life at home was being disrupted to accommodate another person. This feeling was familiar: the tension between honoring myself on one side and doing what I needed to get the love or keep the love on the other side. I still did not feel valuable and lovable just for being me. This makes it so scary to make decisions that fully honor my needs because it feels like I will lose love. Essentially, we are talking about being able to set boundaries, something I wasn't taught growing up. Setting boundaries in the face of the primal panic and fear of losing the love you need is virtually impossible until you understand that you are worthy and lovable no matter what.

I finished packing, loaded the car, and drove an hour to the retreat center. I wasn't mentally prepared in the way that I initially intended. Instead, my mind was trapped in the fear of being unseen, uncared for, unimportant, and unloved/able. My mind was racing, and I was in a complete panic, feeling lost and even more alone than I did before with just my grief.

This, again, was the fear of not-enoughness. This was the thread that drove so much of my actions during childhood and into adulthood. How can I say or do the right things to ensure that I am loved by the people I love? This was my survival mechanism. This part of me sprang into action when it felt like I was going to be abandoned. This was not the magical feeling I wanted to walk into the retreat with me. This was old stuff continuing to plague me. Something I had worked on multiple times in the past that, though healed a bit, still often became triggered and agitated because that part of me believed that I wasn't enough, wasn't worthy, just by being me.

I unloaded the car and tried hard to get into the present moment, which was more difficult than usual with what felt like a gaping soul wound. I began orienting myself to the woods around me, to the cottage we would be staying in for the night, to the smell of the air, and to the magical presence of Ashley. She was there to greet me with a warm hug, her presence calming and steadying. Once I entered the cottage, I found that Ashley had left the itinerary on the bed, along with two roses. Here, in this space, in this moment, I mattered, I was cared for, and my healing and pain were important. I breathed this in and felt it settle over me, even with the undercurrent of survival mechanism and fear.

Rebirth, Release, Rejoice—the name of the retreat and the intention. Ashley and I had discussed ahead of time what I wanted, and this title fully encompassed what I was hoping for. I envisioned emerging from the cocoon of this retreat fully at one with the healing portal, ready to give myself completely to the journey ahead. I got settled in the cottage, and we headed out for dinner in the mess hall. After dinner, we officially opened the retreat with a tea ceremony and closed the evening work with an intention-setting dance around the bonfire. I remember how the night felt walking to the bonfire, like we were the only people in the world. It felt heavy with sacredness, ready to accept and acknowledge our intentions and carry us deeper into the spiritual realm. We danced around the bonfire, releasing what was holding us back and casting it into the flames. The flames danced, higher, lower, brighter, receiving our offerings. We were free and unfettered … mostly. Part of me was stuck in survival and the feeling of being unimportant to my most important person, my husband. Push and pull, I reminded myself to rest back into the Goddess' embrace and asked her to help me release these fears, to show me my value, and to help me to stand confidently in the knowledge of my enoughness. I wrote in my journal, reminding myself that I was not alone; I was loved and accepted, and I belonged. I was held by the Great Mother, held by my mother's spirit and energy. The energetic cords of Goddess held me loosely, stretching to accommodate, allow, and accept all of me. In the acceptance of Goddess, I became aware of all of the ways that being held by the energetic cords of my mom while she was alive didn't allow me to be all of me, didn't allow me to be the fully expressed version of myself. Those cords kept me bound to a cage of smallness, sickness, and a striving for skinniness. I was created to fill a need in my mom to have someone to care for and who could, in turn, care for her and carry all of the emotions for the family.

During the first day of the retreat, I was caught in the familiar tension between anxiety, fear, and honoring my Self: needing to get the love versus honoring my needs and Self. In these moments, it feels as though my very survival is at stake. It is a primal panic and fear. I learned as a child in moments like these that to keep the love around me, I must give in to what the other person wants. Yet, as an adult, I learned that survival in this manner is just that, survival, rather than living in true alignment with my heart, soul, and needs.

This lesson was part of the lesson learned by committing fully to my healing journey. Understanding it and putting it into practice in all the different, scary places it is present are two different things. I was disappointed in my inability to stay present during this retreat due to my triggering survival method. Of course, this was exactly the thing I most needed to lean into differently. This was the opportunity to begin to heal the part of me that felt her value was based on giving another person what they wanted and keeping love at the expense of my own needs, at the expense of my soul.

The anxiety and panic plaguing my mind kept me anchored to the material realm, not allowing me to easily enter an altered state of consciousness and the spirit realm. They kept me tethered to past trauma and created a barrier between me and healing and wholeness. This tether was woven into the tapestry of my soul, yet was a discordant color that did not add to the whole. It took away the harmony and kept me from being all I could be. I know that this was my survival mechanism for my entire life—to try to get it right, to be enough, worthy, valuable, and I would get the love. With my tapestry unraveled due to the loss of my mom, I could zoom out and see that holding tight to this survival mechanism didn't create space for me to thrive and expand fully into my Self. It perpetuated not-enoughness, discordance, and a lack of wholeness.

I went to bed that night and had a tough time sleeping. I tossed and turned, the little girl inside of me stuck in the familiar feeling of being unimportant to my most important person, in this case, my husband. I worried about the state of my marriage, worried that my husband didn't accept me as I was, value me, or think I was important. Those thoughts and the accompanying feelings were devastating. They pulled at me, dragging me into a dark hole, warring with the parts of me that knew there was comfort, love, and acceptance if I could rest into Goddess. This dance of being pulled and ruled by my survival mechanism, wrapped up in trauma from the past and the old thread of not-enoughness, not worthy, and then sinking into the arms of Goddess, releasing into her and being held and loved just as I am was exhausting and kept me from sleep.

The next morning began with meditation on a dock over the water. Sitting there greeting the sun, feeling her early morning warmth on my skin, was exhilarating and calming. It was a wonderful preparation for the day, which would include a tea ceremony, a womb cleansing ritual, and end with a walk of the labyrinth on the property.

My most vivid memories from this day are of the womb cleansing ritual. A womb cleansing ritual is a ceremony intended to help clear the womb of trauma held in the body, both spiritually and energetically. My past is riddled with sexual trauma from an early age. Additionally, the threads that formed the framework of my sexual worldview as a young person and early adult were created from a foundation of not-enoughness, of doing something to be worthy of love. In the case of sex, in my younger years, I believed it was a way for me to be valued, loved, and cared for. This was largely unconscious for me then but had become crystal clear in recent years. These threads were part of the survival mechanism that kept me going throughout my life. This was how I survived the internalized message that I would never be enough, worthy of love by being me. I must find the "right" thing to do to get the love I need to survive and be seen as valuable for something.

From my position, zoomed out and looking at the tapestry that made up my soul, I could clearly see the threads of sexual trauma and discordance related to sex and sexuality woven throughout. They weren't threads I consciously wove. They were a sticky substance mucking up my ability to fully realize my own sexual power.

They kept me entangled and out of flow, grasping and looking for validation. It was time to release these threads, to unweave them. I realized how vitally important it was to heal my sexual wounds and unweave the threads that tied my sexual way of being with trauma and survival rather than pleasure and joy. Cleansing the womb space was my first step toward healing the soul wounds left behind by my sexual trauma history and my sexual survival mechanisms. This ritual opened the portal of healing toward sexual wholeness.

Womb Cleansing Ritual

I wore a red dress. It flowed and swirled around me like water. I was free to move and dance however I felt called. The room was dark even though it was daytime. Ashley lit a charcoal disc in a cauldron and burned incense specifically created for my ceremony, including herbs for cleansing the womb. I squatted over the cauldron and allowed smoke to penetrate me and enter my womb space. It felt strange. The smoke was hot, and it felt like it was burning me, though I knew it was not. I felt awkward, yet I trusted Ashley and Goddess and rested into the flow of their care and love. I called on and released each person who had violated my sexuality in some way. I could feel the presence of my spirit guides, Durga, Sarasvati, others, and now Goddess Isis, who played a big part in the ceremony (and in my life moving forward from this moment). I released all those who had harmed me. The final name on this list was my own. How many times had I violated and betrayed my truth in sexual situations when speaking my truth (saying no) would have risked upsetting those around me, people who I wanted to believe I was valuable, people I wanted to love me or find me worthy. Saying no, even though my body was screaming it, or removing myself from the situation felt impossible to me when getting the love I needed was paramount. My sexual history included so many instances where I did not say no, even though that was the truth ringing through my body and soul. It also included too many situations where I did say no, but it didn't matter. Whoever I was with kept going anyway, as if my voice and I didn't matter at all (which mirrors my experience as a child having her needs, experience, and voice dismissed). After squatting over the smoke and releasing those who had harmed me, we danced. I danced out my pain. I danced in my rebirth. I danced with everything that came and went. I danced.

The womb ceremony left me feeling cleansed and somewhat reborn. It also left me unsettled about the role I played in my own silencing of my voice. The idea that my voice and I didn't matter in the context of heterosexual sex is one of the ways that patriarchy keeps women oppressed and less than. Christ discusses the idea that viewing God as a dominant male allows male domination within a society.[10] Men believing that my "no" holds no value is a way to dominate, to other me, to reduce my value to that of serving them. A reclaiming of the feminine, a settling into Goddess spirituality, allowed me to better understand and see my value and change the force with which I deliver my no.

After the womb cleansing ceremony, we began our closing ceremony at the labyrinth. We called in our intentions for the coming months of healing during the labyrinth walk. I intended to fully step into all that I am, to know I am loved and lovable just as I am, and to know and embody that I am never alone because Goddess is with me. I had come to the retreat expecting a major shift in paradigm, healing, and perspective. I received a gentle opening and

---

[10] C. Christ, "Theological and Political Implications of Re-Imagining the Divine As ...," Political Theology, 2007, https://www.tandfonline.com/doi/abs/10.1558/poth.v8i2.157.

attunement into the major healing coming, of releasing and reclaiming all that I am and anchoring it into wholeness. The intention of fully stepping into all that I am and knowing I am loved and lovable was the theme that would repeat itself in different ways throughout this healing journey. This retreat gently opened the healing portal so that I could step through and begin.

Women's Temple Facilitator Training

In May 2018, AWI offered a training retreat in Colorado to become a facilitator of women's temples. Women's temple is a sacred gathering of women for embodied spiritual practice. It involves movement, sound exclamation, and allowing Goddess to move you and move through you.

It is a safe space to rest entirely in the feminine and be exactly as you are. Having participated in various spiritual practices with AWI the preceding year and longing for a deeper connection to Goddess, my Divinity, and other women, this offering really called me in. I don't necessarily make hasty decisions regarding events like this, but almost as soon as I learned about this retreat, I knew I had to go. I had never been to Colorado before. I would be making this trip alone. I worked out the logistics, found a place to stay, and embarked on this journey that fed my soul.

I was scared. I had traveled alone before, but this felt different. I was unfamiliar with the location and the transportation around the area. I had worked out the public transportation from the airport to Boulder, where the retreat was, but getting to and from the retreat center, I would be relying on a rideshare. Everything felt so unfamiliar to me, and that always makes me nervous. I did it anyway because this retreat called so strongly to my soul.

The journey to Boulder was uneventful. I arrived a day early to get settled and be fresh for the retreat which began the next day early in the morning. It took place in a restored barn on a large farm property owned by another AWI sister. The property was located in a valley, and it was beautiful. Just being on it nourished my soul and brought me peace. In the distance, I could see the mountains, but all around me were grasses waving in the breeze, the sound of a stream rushing over rocks. Had I just gone there to stay and rest in the grass, listening to the stream, I would have found some healing. I went there for training, however, and healing. Such is the nature of learning to work with the Divine feminine and Goddess; the training weaves together with the healing. Everything is experiential and embodied. Upon arrival and check-in, I met another woman working on her doctorate. This immediately helped me to feel less alone.

We gathered in the restored barn, a wide open space with multiple large windows and glass doors. Our lead trainer was a woman named Dominique. Her energy was magnificent. She created a safe container within which we all could fully show up and experience all that there was to experience in the training.

Within this container, we learned how to dance with the Divine feminine and hold space for others in an embodied, loving, and nurturing way. Women's temple is a space with minimal talking and maximal feeling and experiencing. In temple, Goddess moves you. You allow music and feeling to flow through you and express itself in the movement of your body. You allow emotion to come through you and out of you.

Women's temple consists of many different activities designed to help you deepen into your own feminine, your relationship with

Goddess and the Divine, and your relationship with your Self and other women. It is a space to show up as all that you are and be welcomed and held in the embrace of the feminine in all of Her glory. Our temple training lasted five days. I connected with many women in that space, but I connected more deeply with my Self and with Goddess. I began reclaiming the feminine within, though I wouldn't have called it that at the time.

Upon my arrival home, I remember feeling different. I felt a deepened sense of aliveness. I felt a deeper connection to all that I was. It was as though I floated upon the Earth. I felt held by Goddess. I didn't feel alone. There is something profound, I think, about a group of women gathering together to feel, to experience, to be with each other and Goddess. There is something that happens differently when we aren't focused on talking or doing but instead on allowing what is within us to move through us, to move us. As women in a patriarchal society, we don't have many spaces that allow us to just be and experience what is within us in safety. When I returned home, it was with dreams of creating a women's temple locally so that I could share these feelings with others.

Other Trainings

Following the women's temple facilitator training, I participated in two other trainings that felt relevant to my healing and the work I wanted to be doing in the world. I already knew my work was shifting, but I didn't know how yet. I felt called to do more to serve, to somehow bring spiritual healing into my work as a therapist, or to create something separate where I could serve people in this capacity.

To that end, I participated in an Empath Mastery course, having always felt very sensitive and being told I was too sensitive, another way that patriarchy and family used to make me feel not enough. I don't have too much to say about this other than it helped me embrace an aspect of myself that I was previously taught was a weakness. It helped me to see the magical gift of being privy to the emotions of others. It also helped me to create some energy-clearing techniques to use in my therapy practice to help avoid burning out (which I had already had experience with).

The other training I participated in was in Comprehensive Energy Psychology. I attended the conference of the Association for Comprehensive Energy Psychology, which was taking place in Orlando, a short drive away. I remember this conference with great fondness. Something about it helped me feel more embodied, more like my Self. It also could have been the combination of all the healing work I was doing, culminating in a more grounded feeling during this conference. My hope for this conference was to bring this new way of working with energy into my therapeutic work. Although I don't use it explicitly, it has become part of the toolbox I pull from when I work with clients.

Lived Spirituality

Daily spiritual practice was a foundational, vital part of all the healing work I engaged with during this time. It kept me firmly embedded in the healing matrix. It kept me deeply connected to Goddess and my soul and spirit.

During these months of reweaving my shattered soul, I engaged in daily spiritual practice for at least an hour each morning. Most days, this included mantra chanting to Durga and Sarasvati, and working with many different types of crystals. I created crystal grids on and around my body, focusing the energy of the chosen crystals. I did this intuitively, without exploring in advance the properties of the stones I was guided toward. I allowed spirit to guide me in choosing the stones and showing me how and where to place them.

I had always been attracted to stones and crystals. I remember going to quarries with my mom to dig as a child. When she dropped me off at college in North Carolina, we went to a gem mine to find more. Working with crystals unapologetically is one of the aspects of my Self that I reclaimed as I wove myself home to a more aligned and whole version of me.

Daily, I would surround myself with stones during this time of grief and healing, sing mantras, and follow the flow of spirit around me. I would often drop into a journey state and enter the spirit realm. One day, I came into clear contact with a part inside of me that perpetually wanted more, more, more. This was a part of me that felt not enough, and it constantly pushed me to over-effort, work more, and do more so that I could prove my worth and value and get the love I needed to survive.

This time, though, in this particular meditation, on this particular day, I could see this part clearly and vividly, and it could see me. We existed together outside of regular space and time, in the spirit realm of Goddess and healing. I asked it what it needed to help it settle and just be. It answered, "Safety." This sounds simple, yet it was profound. I held this part in my arms and, in my vision, offered it a meal of safety, fed to it with a spoon. I fed it all the safety it could imagine until it was satiated and overfull.

At this point, this part of me became a boon for me—the boon appeared as a smooth-sided, large, clear quartz crystal that represented safety, security, and enoughness. It was mine to keep inside of me as a reminder that I always had those things and could continue to offer them to myself. This was not an easy healing. Interacting with this part was scary in a way I did not often experience when traveling the spirit realm. It was a dark part of me and appeared like a little gremlin. There was nothing soft and welcoming, and it was still necessary for me to hold it, love it, and offer it comfort and safety so that it could feel okay and relax. What a profound lesson in accepting all the parts of the Self, even the dark gremlin parts.

Shinai had suggested that this scenario would present itself, that I would have to attend to a very dark internal wound. This healing took me to a dark place to meet with this part. It was an aspect of my deepest soul wound, the wound of not-enoughness, and what I have come to think of as my life's healing work. It has many layers and shows up in multiple situations in my life. Working with it on this day, in this healing way, shifted it profoundly, but not completely.

After this healing work, I would feel different in my body: safer, more secure, more enough, but I would still get derailed and pulled back into unworthiness. After this one healing journey, however, I became more adept at zooming out when this happened so that I could see what was happening and rest back into the flow around me, rest back into the knowledge that I am enough. I now knew how to offer safety to this part so that it could settle back and relax.

Chapter 5

SURRENDER

Choosing to step through the healing portal and commit to my healing journey was a choice to fully surrender to healing and also to my grief and pain. It was a choice to be vulnerable because letting pain in is vulnerable; creating space for grief is vulnerable … and revolutionary. You might be wondering why I am calling it revolutionary. There are a few reasons.

First, as mentioned many times through this narrative, we live in a culture that pressures us to bury our pain, shove it aside, pretend it doesn't exist, and just get on with business as usual. This is one of the prescriptives of patriarchy and hustle/productivity culture and, for me, the family narrative as well.

Second, even within the context of spirituality, there can be a certain amount of spiritual bypassing along the lines of "positive vibes only." This way of being in the world doesn't allow for the full experience of being human, the wide range of emotions and states, including happiness and sadness, joy and pain, etc. It keeps us fragmented and separate. Vulnerability, letting the pain in, opens a portal to healing, Goddess (or spirit), and everything. It shifts the paradigm from one of separation and fragmentation to one of wholeness. I stopped trying to control things and rested into what was around me and within me. I rested into Goddess' embrace. I realized that vulnerability and surrender were required steps on the journey to wholeness.

Existential Aloneness and the Energetic Umbilical Cord

What happens in your physical body, in your energetic body, when the one being that has been present since before you were born is suddenly gone from this Earth? For me, emptiness. An emptiness the likes of which I had never experienced before. My core felt carved out like a pumpkin without seeds, raw, hollow, jagged. When I paid attention to that emptiness and listened to it, it brought my awareness right to that spot within my body; I felt an energetic cord seemingly attached to my abdomen but free floating on its other end, untethered. This feeling was new, like it had been attached to something before but was cut loose unexpectedly. It floated through the air like a downed electrical wire after a hurricane. It was still a live wire but unattached and floating in the breeze. I felt untethered, as though I were floating like a leaf.

As the grief began to settle within me and I regained some of my realness, it highlighted the felt sense of this energetic cord that was now attached to nothing. I began to refer to this cord as an energetic umbilical cord because that was exactly what it felt like. I realized that it had been attached to my mother's energetic field. With her death, that end of the cord was floating in the air untethered. I was floating in the air untethered. This pain and awareness were a bit more specific than the overall smokiness and insubstantiality I had experienced since her death. I felt it most as an emptiness in my belly and a profound sense of being untethered to anything at all. It felt unimaginably lonely. I named it existential aloneness.

The more I explored and paid attention to this cord, the more I came to understand how this energetic umbilical cord connected me to my mom, perhaps in ways that served her more than they served me. What do you do when your energetic umbilical cord is suddenly floating freely in the air? You reattach it, of course. To what, you might ask? You likely won't be surprised to learn that for me, the answer was Goddess and the great Mother. You could attach it to different aspects of your spirituality or your inner Self, your guides, and your intuition.

With the help of Shinai, I engaged in a ceremony to anchor the energetic umbilical cord deep into spirit, Goddess, the Earth. While in an altered state of consciousness, a deep state of meditation, I took hold of the cord, lovingly caressing it, learning it through touch and curiosity, and listened inside for where it needed to be attached. I followed the internal guidance and saw myself in my mind's eye, anchoring it down into the Earth's energy field, where Goddess could receive it.

During this act, I felt my connection to the world around me restored. I felt Goddess connect and offer succor. In my relationship with my mom, this cord was symbiotic, but it was never intended to be so. As a child, I needed to receive love, safety, and care to survive and thrive unconditionally. It did not serve me to be expected to return that care in the same way or to prove that I was worthy of that care. The cord was intended to provide succor for me, not be symbiotic. Attaching the cord to Goddess put me firmly back into receiving through the cord—love, support, safety, and care.

My mom was my best friend. She was supportive and loving, though not affectionate. Before her death, I would have said that we were very close. After her death, I would say that our closeness was more superficial than I had ever realized. Knowing this creates such profound sadness in my heart. Our closeness was actually a kind of cooperative dependence masked as closeness. After her death, I realized I didn't know her, and I wondered if she knew herself.

Her death showed me things about her, our relationship, our family, and myself that were uncomfortable and invisible to me until she was no longer clouding my vision. In her generation, women were expected to live a certain way, but I don't know if she was ever happy. I know she found joy in me and raising me, but once I was an adult living on my own, where was her joy? I am not sure that she ever found it for herself. I understand now that this has been part of the driving force of dedicating my life to authenticity and wholeness, accepting people just as they are, and creating more acceptance and authenticity in the world. I did not feel I received acceptance or love for being who I am, and I don't feel my mom did either. When I reclaim the authentic parts of myself and work toward being in alignment with wholeness, I thrive. In reclaiming the energetic umbilical cord and rooting it into Goddess, into the Earth, I reclaimed a critical part of sovereignty and authenticity. Goddess doesn't expect anything from me, and she supports me completely. From this place of support, acceptance, and love, I can serve her and myself.

Playing Small

Grounding my energetic umbilical cord into the limitless expansiveness of Goddess helped me to see my expansiveness and showed me the places where I still played small in my life, personally and professionally. I had so many seemingly great ideas over my lifetime that I never fully stepped into.

Since Mom died, I have made many shifts into expansion and could still feel the walls of smallness closing around me. All the bigness that was me was squeezed into a small package, leaving parts cut off and stuck outside the whole. This was a result of my upbringing and also of trauma I experienced in my early teens that left it feeling unsafe to be all of who I was. It was so much safer to take up less space, to be unseen and invisible. Smallness was part of my survival mechanism after sexual trauma as well. The world around me taught me over and over again that to show up as my Self, as my completely bright, shiny me, was dangerous. I learned to shove myself in a box as an adaptation. These walls that I, my culture, and my family placed around me may have helped me survive but also limited my growth and expansiveness.

I began to shift my healing into working on this part of me that felt limited and that still played small, reclaiming the lost soul parts that were shorn away to allow me to play small. Being small was not my nature, my authentic way of being. In a journey/sacred tea ceremony with Ashley, we worked with the Lady of Avalon, who was often present when I worked with Ashley, and her nine crows to collect my missing soul parts.

During the journey, a toad delivered these parts to the holes in my soul. A black panther licked them into place to heal and solidify their place. The panther lay at my side, becoming one of my spirit animals along with the toad. While I am some years removed from this event, I continue to work through healing from playing small. I bump into those manufactured walls periodically that stop me from fully being all that I am. I continue to work with different aspects of this in different ways and attend to each part as it presents itself. It is an ongoing process.

The Feminine

Moving through this journey and studying it, I became aware of how much of my Self, as a woman, was anchored externally. I've mentioned before that patriarchy creates an other focus in us as women. It also raises us to anchor outside ourselves to our partners, careers, kids, and parents who made us. We aren't raised to feel our power and anchor into it in an unshakable way.

Anchoring outside myself taught me that my worth and value were located outside of my Self. Everything hinged on everything else and was all located externally, like a precarious house of cards that could, and did, topple at any moment. My mom's death was not the first experience in my life that left me feeling like I didn't know who I was in the world anymore. I had been through rounds of this work before. Peeling away layers of who society told me I should be, getting closer to who I really was, and finding my worth in my authentic self.

The missing piece every time I had previously done this work was the spirituality piece, the soul healing piece. I didn't address that vital part until this journey of healing after Mom's death. When I anchored anew into Goddess and my Self, I became settled and sturdy in a way I never had been before. For me, this was part of reclaiming the feminine in my Self. It was a reclaiming of my inherent power that I never really knew existed.

The thread of the feminine goes beyond relationship to and anchoring into Goddess. Being raised in a patriarchal society that privileges men and being taught, both by that system and my family system, that my worth relied upon how valuable I was to men also taught me not to value the energetic feminine. The energetic feminine flows and dances with what comes, receives, radiates, softens, nourishes, and embodies.[11] The energetic feminine finds power in flow. Up until now in my life, I did not claim the power of the feminine. I did not understand that it had power. Instead, I cleaved to the energetic masculine of action, of over-efforting. This was the privileged way of being in both family and society, and thus I was out of balance. Reclaiming and reweaving the thread of the feminine back into my tapestry rebalanced my system, helped me be more authentically me, and returned me to a deeper state of wholeness.

As I deepened my understanding of and connection with the Divine Feminine, I reconnected with my body and energetic feminine power. It was a belonging, a homecoming. The feminine has no goal other than maybe presence with the self, spirit, and the Divine. Reclaiming the feminine was the beginning of a reclaiming of all of the parts of my Self.

Soul Parts

What does it mean to become aware of missing parts of the soul? From my shattered, zoomed-out position after Mom died, I could see so much more of my Self. I started to notice missing pieces in my soul's tapestry, missing parts of my soul, my vital essence. It was like looking at the Earth from space and seeing craters or just seeing the missing threads of a tapestry, like when your sweater has a pull and that creates a hole. If I shifted my awareness to those craters, those pulled thread holes, I felt an absence, a sense of loss, and I knew I couldn't continue to walk around fragmented, couldn't continue to walk around without all the parts of my Self intact.

---

[11] Chameli Gad Ardagh, *Come closer: Spiritual awakening for the feminine heart* (Lighting Source Press, 2006).

Through my work as a therapist, I developed my theories about soul loss in the face of trauma or toxic cultural messaging. To me, it seemed as though at the moment of trauma, a part of the soul got stuck in that place at that time. To arrive at healing and wholeness required a reclaiming of those parts lost at those moments of trauma.

That wasn't the only way to lose soul parts, however. Upon reflection, I realized that there were parts of me that I had cut off, parts that I learned were not welcomed by the culture or family around me. To be loved, I jettisoned them, shoved them in a box, detached them from the whole of me. This journey was a journey back to wholeness, however. Reclaiming all of my parts was vital to healing my shattered soul, even though these things weren't directly related to the loss of my mom.

Sexual Trauma

What do I mean when I speak about sexual trauma? If you are a woman reading this, then you likely have your own relationship with the way sexual boundary crossings and sexual safety have played out throughout your life. In short, the way I am using this term describes violations that have occurred to my sexual self in the context of sexuality and my body.

Sexual trauma was a thread that ran through my soul's tapestry from a young age. It took different forms, happened at various ages, and was perpetrated by different people, myself included. I see my past sexual trauma in two different ways. First, times when I said no to sexual activity (or was too young even to know what was happening) and someone did not listen to my no and proceeded despite it, and second, times when my body very clearly screamed a no to me, and I didn't (couldn't) listen, usually because

I didn't want to rock the boat and lose the love that I thought I would receive if I said yes.

You may remember that I mentioned that one of my survival mechanisms throughout my life was to do and be what those around me wanted me to do and be to get the love I desperately needed. I didn't understand (and, of course, survival mechanisms aren't about understanding. They are about survival in the moment in circumstances that feel catastrophic and dangerous) that this was damaging my very essence, disconnecting me from vital parts of my soul. Even if I had understood, I wouldn't (couldn't) have changed anything. This was truly what I thought I needed to do to survive, and I did survive. These two types of violations impacted me differently and required different types of healing.

I realized the first type, violation by others, resulted in a loss of pieces of my soul. They got stuck in the original trauma event. When I looked at the parts of my tapestry, I could see the connection between these traumas and the holes.

This became very clear during a particular sacred tea ceremony. It was a group tea ceremony taking place in Ashley's apartment. I don't remember how many of us were there. It was a small apartment, and having a women's circle there was usually a tight fit. We crowded together on cushions, forming a circle facing Ashley, who poured and distributed tea ritually. I don't remember the purpose of our gathering: a new moon, a full moon, or a holy day of the Wheel of the Year. I knew we were calling in the Goddess Rhiannon, a Goddess of Avalon, a pantheon that hadn't called to me or shown up as one of my guides. I was doing so much healing and spiritual work that the different journeys sometimes run together in my memory.

We settled into a circle, knee to knee, getting comfortable on our cushions. Ashley lit the incense and waved it over the tea, the empty teapot, and the empty tea bowls set in a crescent before her. She was blessing all of the implements of our ritual. We waited in silence. I followed her movements with my eyes, my body already settling in, my mind and spirit beginning to travel to the spirit realm. The ritual nature of her movements and the music around us lulled me and began my journey.

Ashley started to create an image, a place for us to journey. Her words carried us with her to the beach, waiting for Rhiannon to arrive on her white horse. I am strolling along the shore and see her in the distance. She wears a red dress, her hair streaming out behind her, and rides her white horse. Rhiannon gallops toward me and reaches down her hand. I feel no hesitation. This is Goddess at work, who I will always trust, even when it is scary and different. I reach out and take her hand as she pulls me up behind her on the horse. There are no words between us. I am with her, trusting. She is radiant, on fire, beautiful. I don't remember anything else that Ashley said as I was fully lost to the spirit realm, the journey, and Rhiannon. I don't know where we are going, but I trust. She rode us back through time to the first time in my life when I was sexually violated as a young girl. I could see, feel, and witness what happened to that little girl. I saw the pain, fear, lack of safety and trust that the younger version of me felt. I saw the confusion on her face. I experienced this from a distance, as an observer self rather than as that little girl.

At the moment of violation, I saw a part of my soul get trapped in that moment in time, a part of my Self and power stolen from me. This time, though, Rhiannon stepped in just as the soul part was stripped from me. She didn't allow the soul part to be taken or lost. Instead, she restored that part to my soul.

Together, she and I traveled to each event of sexual violation in my past, and as she did for the first event, she stood in the way of the stolen soul part and returned it to my soul. The adult version of me stood by her side and watched her do this and felt each part restored to my soul through time. She stood in each of those rooms and said no and asserted her power to return each of those lost parts to my soul. I began to feel whole in a way that I never had before. I wept at the return of those missing parts of my Self and my power, of my soul. I felt magical. I felt a new sensuality and was aware of my Self and my body in a completely different way. I was reawakened, whole, rooted in Goddess, Earth, and sovereign power. I was rooted in my whole sexuality. I had never experienced this feeling before. I had never viewed sexuality as mine, my pleasure, my joy, my choice. After the final piece of my soul related to sexual trauma was restored, Rhiannon returned me to the beach where she first collected me. I returned to the material realm feeling more whole than ever before.

I had, over the years, done a lot of healing work on my sexual past, but I had never in my life dedicated time solely to healing. I had never surrendered so completely to the process, had never trusted so deeply that Goddess would hold me, heal me, carry me as I did now during this journey. This surrender allowed the healing to be deeper and more intense than ever before.

Leaving that ceremony, I was brimming with newfound wholeness in my soul. I felt drastically different. I was different. Something inside of me was settled, grounded in a way that I had never felt before … or maybe had felt before the age of seven when things went awry. I was comfortable in my skin. The ground was steady beneath my feet. I was reclaiming. While this was profound healing, and I was different, I was still grieving, still healing in other areas, still becoming aware in different ways of the places that needed healing.

The second type of sexual violation, violation by self, was a bit more complicated to parse out and heal. This one was connected to the larger picture of my worthiness and feelings of lovability. If I truly believe that I am lovable and worthy just as I am, then I can say no when no is the right answer for me; I can say yes when yes is the right answer for me. I can be completely me, and those who really love me will still love me. I will still love me. Over my life, there were times when I was in sexual situations where I wanted to say no, wanted to leave the situation, but I just couldn't. I cringed inside, folded in on myself, but was unable to make the no come out of my mouth.

Instead, I separated my spirit from my body, floating above myself, removing myself from the violation that I didn't feel I could stop at the time. As an aside, there is a case here for a lack of affirmative consent. Affirmative consent would have included my partner asking if they could do what they were doing and my saying yes (or no as the case may be), as well as them paying attention to the signals my body was giving (tensing, shuddering, a glazed look in my eyes), and understanding that those signals were not encouragement. None of this happened either, and if I am honest, I still don't know if I would have been able to say no even if asked directly if an action was wanted. I was not taught to say no. I was taught to grin and bear it, not to rock the boat, not upset the apple cart, to turn the other cheek and ignore what was happening. These teachings were compounded by my own experience and internalized messages that I wasn't good enough, worthy, or lovable just by being me. When you gather each of these threads together, the picture they form is one of cowering and being unable to speak up for myself. It is a picture of letting what was happening to me just happen and hoping that the outcome would involve something positive.

I addressed the insidious, underlying thread of unworthiness in a different tea ceremony. In my journal, there is a line that says, "You are always worthy." I have never felt worthy, valuable enough, just by being me. So much of my personal work centered on this foundational wound, and its tentacles spread throughout my lifetime and daily life. It spread into my relationship with food and my body, my relationship to my sexuality, my relationship to spirit, my relationship to my family of origin, my relationship to the culture around me and my place in it, and finally, my relationship to my work in the world as a psychotherapist.

In one of the sacred tea ceremonies I embarked on during my commitment to healing, I envisioned a snake tattoo on my arm. In multiple past life memories, I see myself as an ancient priestess of the Goddess Isis in Egypt. The tattoo in my vision was my priestess mark of that time. It was vivid and representative of feminine power, of my power, of Goddess. It was representative of my journey of healing and wholeness.

When I returned to the material realm after this particular journey, I knew I had to have this tattoo, this physical representation of my commitment to my healing, wholeness, and my relationship with Goddess. It would be a daily reminder of my past lives as a priestess of Isis, of my current commitment to healing and wholeness and flow, and of my work in the world helping others on their journey to authenticity.

Each of my tattoos has always had deep meaning and was an external picture of some journey or deep healing I had embarked on. This was the first time, however, that a tattoo came fully into my life in a vision. I saw it already inked onto my skin, staring up at me. I worked with a tattoo artist to get what was in my head into a picture that would permanently be inked on my arm. Because this is relevant here, I will add that of my nine tattoos at the time, very few of them actually met my expectations. When speaking to the artists historically, I often became nervous and too scared to speak my needs. This wasn't new (as you have learned) but having little pictures inked on my body of times when I couldn't say no or speak my truth was always a reminder of my survival mechanisms and my feelings of not good enough.

The day of the tattoo appointment, I scheduled a tea ceremony with Ashley to ritually cleanse myself and be ready for my priestess mark. Both the Goddess Isis and the God Anubis attended my ceremony in the spirit realm. On the journey, they ritually cleansed my body and applied sacred oils. They bent down to wash my feet. At this point in my vision, I tried to stop them and raise them, indicating that I was the one who should wash their feet as they were Divine beings, and I was, clearly, less-than. Their response was very clear and a bit forceful, indicating that I was worthy of their care, attention, and love, that I was important, enough, all, and that I was also Divine. It was my turn to receive, to surrender, to enjoy. This was not because I did something, offered something of my body, or looked a certain way. This was because I was me, a Divine being in my own right, the Always Worthy.

What did this mean for me? Someone who never felt worthy, who never felt I could be lovable just because I was me? It was a huge exhale, like the world exhaled with me and simultaneously lifted itself off my shoulders. I was the Always Worthy. It was profound healing for me at that moment. Monumental. I was light. I was love. I was a perfect, lovable being in all of my imperfections. Always Worthy settled on my shoulders like a cloak made of sunlight, weightless, alive, empowered, emboldened.

Leaving the ceremony, I made my way to the tattoo shop for my appointment. When the artist took out the drawing of what he was about to ink on my skin, I recoiled. It was nothing like my vision, nothing like I described, and definitely nothing that I wanted to carry on my arm forever. As Always Worthy, I had the strength and confidence to say no, to tell the artist how wrong it was, and to try again to describe how it should be. We rescheduled the appointment. Speaking my truth in that moment would previously have been impossible from my paradigm of "don't rock the boat." In that paradigm, you give, serve, and don't speak your needs. You do not say no. You work to get the love. This shift to Always Worthy loosened the chains that bound me into doing and working for the love I needed. Always Worthy allows me to be more of who I am, to say no when no is warranted, and to say yes when yes is warranted.

Always Worthy is a thread that now lights up the tapestry of my soul. I had been shown again and again by family and patriarchy that I was not good enough. Growing up, when I brought home a good grade or the equivalent accomplishment, congratulations were not forthcoming. Instead, I was met with what I had done wrong and told what I should have done better. This created what I call over-efforting, where I do more, more, more, to prove that I am enough, to get the love that I need to survive, to be worthy of love. I unwove that thread of not enoughness, the thread of over-efforting, and wove in its place the thread of Always Worthy. As Always Worthy, I can rest. I can move with what comes, be present, and flow. I can create. I am lovable just as I am, not at a specific size or with a specific income or because I did a specific thing, like having sex. I am lovable as me.

Chapter 6

DISMANTLING
THE PHYSICAL BOX

In August 2018, almost a year after Mom's death, my husband and I drove to NJ to help my dad pack up the house that I grew up in so that we could sell it. It was too much house for him alone, and I was 65% owner since Mom's death. Her will called for us to put it on the market six months after her death. I was sad. Walking into the same house with the same furniture and the same smells but without my mom's physical presence highlighted her absence again in a gut-wrenching way. It was not that I had forgotten that she was gone, but at home in Florida, she was not a part of my day-to-day living, though I thought of her and wanted to text her constantly.

In NJ, she was that house. She was its heart and soul. My heart hurt. It felt like a weight bearing down on me. I prayed to Goddess to be with me in my pain and leaned into Her embrace. We packed things and separated the things that I wanted, the things Dad wanted to keep, and the things that would be sold in a garage sale when we returned in November. My parents had so many things, including suitcases filled with papers from the 1960s! It was an excessive amount of work and largely fell to my husband and me to complete it. This work, this dismantling in the material realm, was a further dismantling of the structure that was my mother, my past, and the cage and scaffolding she built for me. I felt as though I was continuing to pick out my mother's threads that were still woven into the tapestry of my being.

During this time, my husband and I began running. We needed to get some of this emotional baggage and stress out of our bodies. It was stagnant, and we needed to shake it off like a dog shakes off a scare. Exercise for me historically had been driven by my disordered eating, by my need to be skinny and, thus, lovable and worthy. Exercise obsession has always played a part in this.

This new running practice was different. I set parameters. Knowing my triggers, I allowed myself to run only three times per week, and I changed my intention. I was running to run, not to be faster or go longer to be skinnier. The part of me that had always called for more, more, more was quiet, satisfied with its previous meal of enoughness and safety. The part of me always wanting to be thinner, thinking that thinner equated to being loved and lovable, was also quiet. This was not to say that I never heard these parts anymore. They had a long history of leading me and helping me survive by pushing me toward things they thought would get and keep love, like being a certain size.

Now, though, we were working together toward health and wholeness, toward unapologetic authenticity and intrinsic worthiness. This was the new foundation from which I moved through the world. From this foundation, I realized something was missing from my healing work and engagement with wholeness … my body.

I thought that my care of myself was holistic. Having been trained as a yoga instructor and a transpersonal, holistic, systems-oriented psychotherapist, I had an idea in my head that I looked at the entire picture of myself when I addressed healing. Intellectually, I understood the connection between mind, body, spirit, emotions, energetic body, and soul, but I realized that I wasn't actually living up to my ideals of wholeness. As I moved deeper into my healing journey, I realized that there were parts of myself not getting the healing and attention that they needed as part of my system.

From the age of 25, I have dealt with chronic illness. I tried to fix what was broken in my body through modern medicine, in keeping with the way the medical model views illness as a separate part to be fixed in the body, without looking at the whole. As much as I tried to make this method work, it just didn't. It wasn't until a few years ago that I realized the importance of looking at the whole in relation to my physical dis-ease. Once I added spirituality to my self-care and nourishment practices, my health began to shift.

In the months following my mom's death, I kept feeling like I had a cold. For the first year, as I've mentioned, I went through a two-week cycle where I felt like I was getting sick, was sick, or was getting over being sick over and over again. A part of me was frustrated with this cycle, but the majority of me understood this to be related to grief and healing moving through my body.

Since I was not working at the time and was fully focused on my healing, this cycle didn't interrupt my daily living much, though nothing about it felt good. I also felt as though I had no control over my body (do we ever?), and that felt disconcerting and destabilizing. I was already focused intensely on my healing. I did not, however, rest into the illness and get curious about it as I did with most other things: emotions, feelings, resonances, and intuitions that came up. Instead, I ignored it. I continued to treat the body as other, something that needed fixing or something to ignore since I seemingly had no control over it. I have learned over time that when I do not process my emotions, they show up in my body as physical illness. I believe that this is partly why I have always struggled with physical dis-ease. There was no safe space for my emotional experience as a child, thus it got stuck in my body and showed up as illness, something much more acceptable to the family system and culture around me as I grew up. I also learned, through uncomfortable experiences, that my body keeps talking, even when I do not stop to hear it. Especially when I don't stop to listen to it. Then, it speaks louder in ways that demand attention, like an illness that renders me physically dysfunctional.

This time, my body was yelling at me through this cycle of perpetual illness. I wasn't listening well enough. It had to yell louder to get my attention. Parts of me started to hurt, particularly my right foot, which had had a bunion for my entire adult life. My mom and my grandmother both had one as well. Mine was exacerbated by many years of wearing heels to look sexier, more desirable, and to get love. By this point, I was often in a lot of pain, especially when standing or walking for long periods of time. I had stopped wearing heels, but the damage was done. Then, I stubbed my toe, and the pain increased significantly. The pain in my foot impacted my knee and my hip and even contributed to my cervical spine being out of alignment. What an amazing example of the connectedness of everything (though a painful one!). These details led me to add body work to my healing endeavors.

This was the first time in my life I had focused on healing all the different aspects of my whole. I feel like it should have been obvious from the beginning, but it wasn't, and it happened at exactly the time it needed to happen when I was ready for this particular integration.

Structural integration works from the feet up, so from the first session, I felt a profound difference in my level of foot pain. I was doing so much work to reclaim my missing soul parts but not doing the work to move my body into deeper wholeness and alignment. Finally, I learned it was impossible to do the work of releasing, reclaiming, and stepping into deeper authenticity and wholeness without attending to the body. Bringing in the body was one of the missing pieces of the healing and wholeness puzzle for me. My body and I had a rough relationship for most of my life. I did not nourish it well enough because of body image issues. I treated it as an object to be changed, to be fixed, frustrated by, to acquire love through sex. I didn't treat it as the miraculous part of me that it is. While I was already healing my relationship to food, I wasn't working on healing my relationship to my body. Structural integration opened the door wider for me to see my body and love it differently and just as it is.

During the recent pandemic of 2020 (and 2021 and 2022 …), I added another body-healing activity to my healing practices: nervous system energy work. This work happens remotely and helps to calm the nervous system. I have experienced profound shifts in my physical well-being since adding nervous system energy work. This work also requires that I maintain a deep connection with my body and pay attention to what is happening inside me. The integration of my structure allowed for a deeper integration of all the healing work I was engaged in.

One Year Since Mom's Death

October 2018 brought the culmination of a lot of the work I was doing internally, in body and soul, and milestones in the material world as well. Over the summer, I submitted a proposal to present my story of healing at the Women Rising conference held by the California Institute of Integral Studies in San Francisco. I truly believed that speaking and performing the story of my healing journey had the power to move others toward healing, and that is what I proposed to do in my presentation.

This would be the first time that I had presented at any conference. I was nervous and also excited. This journey of healing, of reweaving my soul into wholeness following my mom's death, was deeply personal, and I felt that it had something to offer others. It felt imperative to stand in that conference and share with others. Writing that presentation was the first time I wrote this story, or at least parts of it. I'm not sure I knew then that it would become my dissertation and this book. I just knew that I felt compelled to write and share it. The story, as I wrote it at that time, was about the acute stages of grief and the healing power available when I rested into my relationship with Goddess. I hadn't fully studied my journey yet, so my understanding of it was limited to this small foundational part. This part was vital, however. Without this foundation, without Goddess to hold me, I would have struggled considerably more.

October 2018 was also the one-year anniversary of my mom's death. Greek tradition requires a church service and luncheon to honor the deceased. My husband and I flew to NJ for this event and to help pack up the rest of the house I grew up in and have a garage sale. We had accepted an offer to sell, and my dad hadn't packed. I don't have much to say about the church service or luncheon. They were understandably sad but felt very different than the funeral the year before. I was more grounded, more whole, less insubstantial. I found joy in seeing and connecting with my cousins and extended family again. I did not speak at the luncheon, just as I did not speak at the funeral service. At the funeral, I felt that I could not be coherent. My grief overwhelmed my speech. At the one-year memorial, I did not know what to say. The nature of my relationship with my mom and our shared, passed-down trauma responses had, by this time, been held up in a stark light. I always thought I knew my mom and that we were close, but I learned that I was close to the version of her that I saw, not the hidden, authentic one. She loved me immensely, of that I have no doubt, and I, in turn, loved her immeasurably. I understood now how much she carried the expectations of others and society because I had carried them too. They were woven throughout us, whispering about our worth and keeping us from being authentically us. Who might she have been if she could have been truly and authentically her? This is part of where my passion for this work of authenticity comes from. I believe you deserve to live life as you truly are, not from the cultural or familial scripts laid out by those around you. My mom would have been such a shining light of magic because I know her love felt that way to me. It saddens me that she never got to live authentically in her wholeness and that our relationship didn't have the depth available to two authentically loving and living women. I miss what I had with her, and a part of me longs for what I never had. She played small, defined by marriage and motherhood, yet she had a master's degree in education. She needed me to play small, to need care, to need her. I am grateful for the relationship that we did have though, and will never stop missing her.

It feels important to mention here that my experience and understanding of my mom's and my inauthenticity, conforming to society's "shoulds" to be found worthy, are huge drivers in my mission to increase unapologetic authenticity in the world. My mom's magic was stifled under societal expectations, and for much of my life, mine was as well.

This is true for so many women in our culture. I truly believe we can begin to heal the world by unraveling patriarchy and societal shoulds from our souls' tapestries and stepping powerfully into our unapologetic authenticity. The world needs our individual authentic magic. It needs us to play big in all of our glory.

Packing up the house for the upcoming sale was torturous. I didn't expect it to be any different, though I did expect that my dad would have done some of it before we arrived. We had a whirlwind few days after the memorial to prepare an entire house full of 48 years of my parent's lives, and my own, for a garage sale, pack my dad up to move, and empty the rest of the house. It was a tall order. It was a depressing situation. It was exhausting in every way: physically, mentally, emotionally, and spiritually. And we didn't finish what we needed to do. It necessitated another (third) trip to NJ in December to move my dad into his apartment and finish emptying the house. That third trip was equally stressful and depressing, and even after that, we dumped so much of their possessions into a storage facility. I fully believed that this was kicking the can down the road for me to deal with upon my father's death, but at the time, we did the best we could with the time and energy we had.

Back to Work

In January 2019, I returned to my psychotherapy practice. Finally, I actually felt ready to go back to holding space for my clients. My healing journey was not over, but it was now becoming integrated into my daily life. I returned to sitting in front of clients as a different person, more deeply my Self. This changed how I saw therapy and how I saw my work as a therapist. The importance of soul work to therapy work was highlighted for me, as was the vital need for the therapist to engage in their personal healing journey. This was my understanding of being a whole-person therapist. It is standing in grounding relationship with wholeness and authenticity and helping my clients to create their own relationships with wholeness and authenticity.

A lot of the work I was doing during this time was around dancing with what comes: allowing what arises to arise, being in the flow rather than over-efforting. This is where my school writing and journal writing were also focused. I had been taught to over-effort, to do more, *more,* **more,** to prove my worth and value and get the love. Shifting into flow and allowance was a distinctly different paradigm. The foundation of this paradigm was knowing my intrinsic worth and value, understanding that I am valuable and worthy because I am me, not because I do more. My healing journey did not finish here; it became more of a light flow than the torrent it was during that first year, focused solely on healing. There was a tension between the old operating system of not-enoughness and the new one grounded in worthiness. I had worked deeply on the core of me, and now the work widened into rings around me that increased in size. The ripples moved outward from my core changes like a still pond disturbed by a thrown pebble, healing the peripheral rings and coming back again to the core, to wholeness, authenticity, flow, and spirit.

Chapter 7

CHOOSING AUTHENTICITY... AGAIN

As I write this book, transforming my dissertation, it's been almost six years since my mom died. Some of the preceding years were spent at home and away from people due to the coronavirus pandemic. During that time, I wrote my way into more and deeper healing by studying my healing journey and writing my dissertation about it.

Since Mom's death took place in the first semester of my doctoral program, it shaped all my graduate work that followed. It has also become a major event point in my life. When I think about events in my mind, they take place either before Mom died or after. I believe that my writing during graduate school played an integral part in my healing and understanding of my internal landscape. I worked on the beginning aspects of my dissertation during the spring, summer, and early fall of 2020 and completed data collection in mid-December. As I embarked on analyzing and writing this story, I deepened my understanding of all I became during the journey. More importantly, I deepened my understanding of the process I went through to heal. As I have written it again now, transforming it from a dissertation to a book that hopes to move you, I have deepened my understanding yet again.

Ch-Ch-Ch-Changes

This book documents most of my internal changes as a result of my healing journey. There have been some notable external changes as well, most prominently in my psychotherapy practice. Embarking on my personal healing journey highlighted the importance of the soul in therapy and the therapist's own healing journey. I have dubbed this model The Whole Person Therapist Model.

My mother's death provided an inheritance that allowed me to move forward with my dream for my psychotherapy practice to be a center for authenticity and healing. My new understanding of the critical factors in the therapeutic process—soul and the therapist's healing journey—informed my mission and values creation for a group psychotherapy practice. The practice's mission was to provide therapy for those who have never felt allowed to be themselves by culture, family, and/or trauma. The center was called The Center for Wholeness. Each therapist I hired was grounded in their healing journey as the foundation for their lives and how they show up as therapists in the room with clients. There was a huge learning curve for me as I created this center and vision, and of course, I struggled with my tendency to over-effort, to do more, more, more, to be worthy. I continued to remind myself to rest back into the embrace of Goddess, rest back into the flow, knowing that I am always worthy.

What Do I Truly Want?

It might seem like our story ends here, but I am learning that there is always space for more healing and deeper authenticity. I mentioned above that it was my dream to open a center for authenticity and healing, but I'm not sure that is strictly true. It is my mission to increase authenticity and wholeness in the world, to help women fully meet themselves and stand in the power of unapologetic authenticity, unraveling patriarchy and society's shoulds from the inside out. I interpreted that to mean that I needed to run a center, but after four years of leading the group practice, The Center for Wholeness, I was burned out and felt like my soul was being eaten alive.

We were wildly successful. During the pandemic, we grew quickly. I made some missteps, particularly with some mis-hires, and I learned that I struggle with firing people who need to be fired. I filled all the offices with some great therapists (and some not-so-great ones). I was able to phase myself out of direct clinical work, which is what I wanted, right? But wait a minute ... I am uniquely qualified to guide people toward their deeper authenticity. I have lived in this realm for much of my life, and I have the education and experience of doing this for others for many years as well. Did I want to phase myself out of clinical work? What is it that I truly wanted? I plugged along running the practice, thinking I would finally have the time and money to shift my work into soul coaching and writing (this book!). But the practice ate all my mental, physical, and emotional energy, leaving nothing for me.

During the summer of 2022, I had three therapists give notice over three months. That was half our clinical staff! When I received the third one, I sat stunned at my kitchen table. I didn't move or speak. I stared out the window and began deeply exploring what I truly wanted (again!). Did I want to rebuild this? Was it time to cut ties, close the practice, and fully launch into my heart's passion? I knew by this point that running a practice and managing people was not the deepest mission of my heart and soul. I felt in my bones that I wasn't reaching my full potential and wasn't fulfilling the mission set for me by Goddess. I was stuck in the dirt, down in the trenches, mucking, but not actually helping people heal, using my knowledge and expertise. It was time for a change … again. It was time to burn it all down. I can't say that this was an easy decision, nor was it easy to stay the course once I made the decision. I knew, though, that this would free me to serve the world from my heart and soul more deeply.

When I started the group practice, I thought about two things: reaching more people, thus increasing authenticity in the world, hiring more therapists, and increasing my income so that I could be free to pursue my soul coaching and writing business. Running the practice required wearing every hat in the business, however: marketing, managing people, selling, accounting, networking, emptying garbage, website updates, SEO updates, and social media management. Everything that you can imagine, and some things you can't, fell to me. I began to delegate to administrative assistants, but it was still too much, and the stress of thinking about it nearly buried me. This definitely wasn't what I wanted to be doing. It wasn't what I was called to be doing. It wasn't authentic to who I was.

Deciding to close the practice was both very hard and very easy. I made the decision pretty quickly, by the end of the day I received that third notice of someone leaving, but I was terrified. My stomach was in knots, and my brain was fuzzy. This would seriously impact my income, which pokes at the part of me that is used to feeling like income and productivity equal my worth and value. I had to give space to that part of me that was scared and that connected productivity to worth. I also had to drop back into the healing I had already experienced of unweaving that thread and releasing it from my tapestry. This throwback to how I used to show up in the world was a great reminder that this isn't how I need to show up anymore. I have untangled the thread of worth related to productivity and could rest into the always worthy once again. I understand that healing isn't linear. Though I have released this thread, there are times that something pokes at the shadow of it and invites the way I used to be to come forward. During those times, like this one, I can very intentionally rest back into what I know now to be true rather than being ruled by the threads that were woven into my being by my trauma, my family, or the culture around me.

Having decided to close the practice, once again choosing authenticity, I informed the staff and began the logistical process of unraveling a business that I had given my heart and soul to for over four years. It was humbling and terribly sad. I felt like a failure even though I knew I wasn't. I had consciously decided to take care of me and my needs. I went through a grieving process, a letting go process, and another, different healing process.

The truth was, I was truly burned out. For the first few months after the closing, I rested and recovered my mental, emotional, and physical well-being. And then, in January 2023, I hit the ground running, starting this book and beginning to create a coaching business dedicated to helping women come home to themselves, step into their unapologetic authenticity, and finally feel good enough ... guiding others to their Always Worthy. When I say I hit the ground running, I mean in some ways I sank back into over-efforting, something I am so familiar with. Then I again found my way back to the truth of who I am and my always worthy and let go a little bit.

This new business has transitioned once already as I continue to deepen into my authentic self and truly get aligned with my soul's purpose. This time around I am doing it in a way I never have before. It is deeper, more whole, more authentic. It is grounded in spirit and soul and not driven by money or the need for love. Goddess breathed it through me and into the world, into you.

Chapter 8

A RECAP

When I began my healing journey after Mom died, I had no idea where it would take me. I thought I was healing my grief, or at least giving it space to be how it needed to be. This was true, but in actuality, I did so much more. My mother's death broke me in a way I never expected, but it also opened a portal to healing the likes of which I never could have anticipated. This allowed me to see more of the threads of my soul's tapestry from a zoomed-out perspective, partly because it completely unraveled the tapestry of me, and thus, it allowed me to attend to them in ways that offered deeper healing than I had ever experienced before.

Walking through this healing portal allowed me to release things that didn't serve me, reclaim things I had lost due to life, and anchor them all home in a new and deeper wholeness. It allowed me to heal things that had defied healing for the length of my life, such as my thread of disordered eating and my relationship with my body. This journey helped me to release the thread of feeling not good enough and unworthy of love and replace it with a thread of always worthy. I was able to reclaim parts of myself that were cut off due to sexual trauma and deepen into the wholeness of me.

The Soul's Tapestry

The healing work outlined in this story illustrates my inner, spiritual work to recreate, reclaim, release, reorient, and re-form my tapestry into a more whole, more authentic version of me. Some threads that were previously part of my tapestry were healed or deliberately released and left behind because they weren't mine and didn't serve me. Some other threads were reclaimed or claimed for the first time.

I visualize this as a large tapestry woven of different threads and colors, some vibrant and glistening, some dark, some harmonious, some discordant. This was the tapestry of me. Some threads were woven into it by the culture around me, some by my family of origin; some were created and woven through the tapestry by trauma, my own and that passed down from my parents and their parents before them. Some threads were created and woven in as survival mechanisms by me post-trauma. Glistening throughout that tapestry was also the color that fully represented my authentic essence, soul, and spirit.

When I speak of being shattered by Mom's death, I visualize that shattering as an unraveling of the tapestry of me. Each thread that was a part of my known whole now floated in the wind, untethered, unwoven. Many of these threads belonged to my mother. They were woven through my being as she raised me. With her death, those threads were pulled, unraveling the entire thing and allowing me to see the threads more clearly, to see what was disharmonious in the tapestry and what was harmoniously mine.

The journey that I embarked on, beginning with my decision to lean into grief, was a reweaving of my tapestry. In this reweaving, I unwove and released threads that were culturally and socially forced into my tapestry but that weren't true to me. I healed and unwove threads of my parents' trauma, threads of my own trauma and survival mechanisms, threads from my family of origin that did not serve me. I rewove parts of my soul that had been missing due to trauma in the past. I rewove threads that were lost to playing small. I rewove the thread of the feminine that was rejected for survival in a male-dominant culture. I rewove all the authentic parts of myself into a new tapestry. The new tapestry was a more whole, more authentic me.

Wholeness

I've mentioned a few times that this journey helped me attain a greater feeling of wholeness within myself. I've realized that wholeness, for me, was more than a reclaiming of the parts of my Self lost to trauma, for survival, or due to culture or family upbringing. Wholeness was also a releasing, or unweaving, of the obligations and expectations of the culture and family around me that didn't align with who I am. It was a shedding of the chains that bound me, and the threads woven into the tapestry of me by others, especially my mom, and by the culture around me, the threads that were disharmonious to my authentic soul. It was a stepping out of, and a releasing of, the roles that were created for me in my family structure and cultural structure and a stepping into my unapologetic authenticity.

Threads Unwoven

In her book *Playing Big,* Tara Mohr discussed the internal effects for women of living under the system of patriarchy, from years of being excluded from politics, business, and professional life. The behaviors she outlined that women have adopted to survive closely resemble what I call playing small in my own life. Playing small is how I showed up in the world prior to my healing journey. These behaviors included "conflict avoidance, self-censoring, people-pleasing, tentative speech, and action."[12] From a young age, all of these behaviors were how I showed up in the world to get the love I needed and prove my worthiness in society. These threads were prominently woven into my tapestry by culture and family and compounded by trauma that showed me how dangerous it was to show up as my full, vibrant, authentic self. These threads were disharmonious to my soul and the threads of my essence but did the job of helping me to survive. I had tried many times to heal these threads (not knowing they were threads) during my lifetime using therapy, but it didn't go deep enough. It didn't get to the heart of the matter. I never understood why, though, and couldn't figure out what wasn't working. After Mom died, I could see so much more of my tapestry, and that bird's eye view showed me what needed to happen to truly heal. Once I saw that some threads woven into my tapestry were discordant and not part of my essence, I could unweave them. The thread of playing small, of working to prove I was lovable, enough, and worthy, was woven throughout my tapestry by both family upbringing and patriarchal society.

Patriarchy

The system of patriarchy created a web of chains surrounding me and infiltrating my very soul's tapestry. It limited me, held me back, and kept me constantly feeling less than, not enough. It pushed me to prove my worth and value to get the love I needed (that we all need) to survive in our society. It told me I existed to serve

---

[12] Tara Mohr, *Playing Big: Practical Wisdom for Women Who Want to Speak up, Create, and Lead* (New York: Avery, an imprint of Penguin Random House, 2015), p. xxviii.

men sexually, physically, and emotionally. Gilligan and Snider said that patriarchy is a system that "forces a split between the self and relationships so that in effect men have selves, whereas women ideally are selfless, and women have relationships, which surreptitiously serve men's needs."[13]

This was certainly my experience of growing up as a woman in a patriarchal society. I was not taught to value my Self, my experience, to stand up for myself. I was taught to focus on the other. During this healing journey, I began to clearly see all the ways that the patriarchal system within which I was chained impacted my life and made me less, and I could, finally, unweave those threads. This is not to say that they are forever unwoven from my system. I still live in a patriarchal society, but I am much more able to see when one of these discordant threads has woven itself back into my way of being in the world, and I can release it again and step more confidently and powerfully into my power and worthiness.

Disordered Eating

One of the threads that plagued me throughout my life was the thread of disordered eating. I didn't always know that that was what I was dealing with. This became more clear as I got older and became a more experienced therapist. This part of me defied healing. After Mom died, I could clearly see that this disordered eating thread was actually hers and wasn't mine to carry. I could see that the origin of this thread was in my mom's history of being called "fatty" by her family and learning about her worthiness as a woman. This thread was also connected to the threads of patriarchy and playing small

---

[13] Carol Gilligan and Naomi Snider, *Why Does Patriarchy Persist?* (Cambridge, UK: Polity Press, 2018), p. 6.

because being thin meant being desirable, worthy, valuable, and lovable, and meant I could get love. On my healing journey, I could do the work to release this thread and finally heal this part of myself. Once I could see that this thread didn't belong to me and its root was actually attached to my mom's tapestry, I could choose to let it float away, leaving me with the space it left in my tapestry and the ghostly reminder of its presence. Understanding that this wasn't mine to carry, that it was mom's in origin, made it easier to heal and unweave from my tapestry.

Living this story and the exploration that followed highlighted the various cultural chains and threads that kept me stuck and kept me from being fully my Self. This journey allowed me to heal wounds related to them, letting them dissolve in the wind and not weaving them back into my tapestry. This story illuminated the chains of culture and family that created me and were woven into the very essence of me, yet weren't my inner truth. To be in the deepest relationship with my wholeness, I had to choose to let go of, to unweave, the threads of my tapestry that didn't serve me and weren't in alignment with my true authentic self, like threads of patriarchy and threads whose origin was my mom's trauma. These threads were discordant. In my mind's eye, they were a color that did not match the threads of my essence. Upon her death, they stood out starkly to my inner vision, and those threads that were impossible to heal previously finally became knowable and touchable.

Threads Rewoven

Equally important to the threads unwoven and released were the threads and parts reclaimed or claimed for the first time in my life and woven into a more whole, more authentic tapestry of me. These included parts of my soul that I reclaimed that were lost to trauma, threads of the sacred feminine, and the vibrant thread of me as the

Always Worthy. What I had never realized before this particular journey to authenticity was that my tapestry had missing parts, blank spots, where parts of my Self were cut off and jettisoned, due to trauma or trying to fit in in a world that wanted me to be someone that I am not. This healing work allowed me to *see* those holes, attend to them, and claim more of my damn Self.

What is also clear to me as I write this is that the field that the tapestry lies in is the field of spirit. None of this work would have been possible without my living relationship with Goddess and my lived spirituality. She was the very air that sustained me and became a prominent thread in my tapestry that took up some space left by the absence of my mother's thread. Perhaps not a thread but the very warp that the pattern of me was woven through.

Stolorow discussed that a field of relational holding was required to fully process emotions related to trauma. In this relational field, there was space for the trauma and anxiety to fully integrate, which allowed the survivor of trauma to move into a deeper authenticity. Without this relational field, the traumatized individual was more likely to shift into what I call business as usual, described by Stolorow as numbing themselves from emotions.[14] My lived relationship with Goddess was this relational holding field for me. This field allowed me to choose to fully lean into my grief, accepting the vulnerability inherent in this action, thus moving toward greater integration, authenticity, and wholeness.

Soul Parts

My story explored some of my personal work to reclaim my soul parts lost to trauma earlier in my life, accompanied by the Goddess

---

[14] R.D. Stolorow, "Identity and Resurrective Ideology in an Age of Trauma," Apa PsycNet, 2009, https://doi.org/10.1037/a0015487.

Rhiannon. As she interjected herself into the scene before I lost my soul parts, during each sexual violation, the soul parts restored themselves to that younger version of me. This healing carried forward through time to the present, allowing me to feel a sense of wholeness in my sexual self, in my very soul, that I had not felt for a very long time. Restoring these lost soul parts was reweaving threads of my soul throughout my tapestry. This filled some of the blank spaces in the tapestry of me. Blank spaces that I was completely unaware of even though I was aware of and had even worked to heal my sexual trauma in the past.

The Feminine

As noted previously, my lived spirituality and relationship with Goddess was the relational field surrounding me that allowed me to engage in this healing journey. Goddess also showed me that I was a Divine being. I could see this as I awakened to a relationship with Her. In Her, I saw the Divine in a female form, something foreign to how I was raised, which was in service to the masculine, in service to me. I was raised as a Christian and taught to revere God the Father. I was taught that I was less-than, not enough, not worthy, not Divine.

The thread of the feminine goes beyond the relationship to Goddess, however. Being raised in a patriarchal society that privileges men and being taught that my worth relied upon how valuable I was to men also taught me not to find value in the energetic feminine. The energetic feminine flows and dances with what comes, receives, radiates, softens, nourishes, and embodies.[15] The energetic feminine finds power in flow. I did not claim the energetic femi-

---

[15] Chameli Gad Ardagh, *Come closer: Spiritual awakening for the feminine heart* (Lighting Source Press, 2006).

nine throughout most of my life. Instead, I cleaved to the energetic masculine of action and over-efforting, of doing more, *more,* **more** to be valuable. These are traits that have more value in a patriarchal society. This was also a more acceptable way to be in my family. I was out of balance and had cut off the thread of the feminine. Reclaiming and reweaving the thread of the feminine back into my tapestry rebalanced my system and helped me become more authentic and whole.

The Always Worthy

In a journey to the spirit realm with the Goddess Isis and God Anubis, I was shown that I am the Always Worthy. Previously, I experienced a life where this was not the dominant message I was taught by family or culture. I was taught that I was not good enough. When I arrived home with a good grade or something similar, congratulations were not forthcoming. Instead, I was met with what I had done wrong and what I could do next time to be better. This created within me a tendency to over-effort, to do more, more, more, to prove that I am enough, to get the love that I needed to survive, to be worthy of love. I unwove the thread of not-enoughness, the thread of over-efforting, and wove in its place the thread of Always Worthy, the phrase given to me by Goddess. If I am the Always Worthy, I can rest when needed. I can move with what comes, be present, and flow. I am lovable just as I am. This thread lights up the tapestry of me.

The Body

Historically, I ignored the information I received from my body to my detriment. My over-efforting frequently pushed my body beyond its limits, leading to physical illness. My disordered eating and exercise obsession also contributed to chronic illness. Finally, my learned behavior of not resting into my emotional pain, of not allowing it to exist and processing it, of continuing with business as usual, also manifested in frequent and chronic illness.

I learned through this healing journey that I needed to weave the thread of the body back into my tapestry. This meant extending my healing exercises to bodywork in addition to spiritual healing. When I began to do this, all the healing work I was doing integrated deeper. This thread of the tapestry was one of the threads that unified and held all the threads in place, much like the body houses all of me.

To weave this body thread back into my tapestry, I first had to unweave the threads of my disordered eating and over-efforting. This created space for the thread of the embodied body to exist, and it also created space for the body-healing thread to tighten the weave of my tapestry.

The tapestry is the system of me, of my soul. To reach my full potential as a human being, to be fully authentic, and in relationship with my wholeness, it required first seeing the tapestry and all of its threads. This was a zoomed-out seeing but also a deep and vulnerable seeing. It required looking and noticing what doesn't fit, what isn't mine, and committing to removing those threads. It also required a willingness to see what wasn't there, the missing parts, the holes in the essence of me, and doing the work to reclaim all of those parts of my Self I may not have wanted to look at. Finally, I anchored the tapestry deep into my body and into the relational field with Goddess, feeling grounded and complete.

CONCLUSION

As a result of this journey, I have emerged with a deeper understanding of who I am now, without a mother in this world, a deeper connection to my lived relationship with Goddess, and a new method for helping others reweave the tapestry of their souls into wholeness and unapologetic authenticity. I have also clearly come to see the threads of patriarchal culture and family culture and how they shaped me and worked hard to keep me from reaching my full potential as a human being and as a woman.

Despite doing this level of deep work, I can still sometimes feel the shadows of the newly unwoven threads in my tapestry, especially since I remain living in a patriarchal system. However, these ghostly threads are more obvious to me, and I can choose how to respond and act when they are present. The way that I live my life has changed fundamentally. I live loudly and shiny, knowing that I am Always Worthy. The way that I practice therapy has shifted immensely to include an emphasis on the therapist's healing journey and to include helping people reweave the parts of themselves lost to trauma in the past.

Possibly the biggest external change I've experienced is how I serve the world. I have long called myself a warrior for authenticity. Moving through this journey and obtaining firsthand knowledge and experience of the deep soul work of weaving and unweaving authentic and not-so-authentic threads has grounded my work with authenticity in a much deeper, more profound way. Authenticity is the magical elixir, the antidote, for so much of our suffering. We live in a world that tells us who we should or should not be and does not allow us the space to learn and live as who we really are.

Living out of alignment with your authenticity increases anxiety and depression and is downright exhausting. It is constantly wearing a mask and playing a part, shoving down who you really are and your true desires and needs. Increasing authenticity in the world is my calling. I truly believe that the more authentic we are, the more we reclaim our lost parts and unweave those threads that don't serve us, the more we will experience health and well-being and a reduction in suffering.

Because I know in my heart and soul that it is my mission, my spirit-directed mission, to help others find their way home to their unapologetic authenticity, it was vital for me to understand what I did to heal during my journey. Exploring and investigating my healing allowed me to create coaching programs designed to guide you through your own healing journey.

I have often claimed over the years that my superpower is the ability to zoom out and see these patterns in the soul's tapestry or the system around us, like patriarchy or the family system in which we were raised. Using this superpower allowed me to see more of myself and allows me to see more in my client's tapestries as well. From this perspective, I can help them heal and find their way home to themselves. Perhaps the most crucial factor in allowing me to embark on such a profound healing journey was that my mom's death completely unraveled the tapestry of me.

What would it be like for you to release those threads woven into your tapestry by culture, family, or trauma that aren't yours, that pull you away from your inner truth, your shining light? Have you wondered how much of you isn't true to you? I invite you to embark on your own journey of finding your way home to your true Self, shedding the chains of family and patriarchy holding you back from your full potential so that you can stand proudly and powerfully in your unapologetic authenticity. You are also Always Worthy.

YOU'VE READ THE BOOK, NOW JOIN THE REVOLUTION

Ready to ditch the labels and unleash your true self? Join my **5-day Soulful Spark Challenge** (and my email list!) and embark on a transformative journey that will leave you feeling empowered, aligned, and unapologetically YOU. This is your first step to redefine your boundaries, amplify your voice, and spark your soul. Sign up now, and let's ignite your inner revolution!
emytafelski.ck.page/spark

Visit my website: emytafelski.com

Intrigued by my work and ready to go even deeper than the email challenge? Want to start your own journey of releasing what doesn't serve you, reclaiming your personal power, and standing strongly in your unapologetic authenticity? Start your revolution by booking a Soul Ignition (discovery) call:
emytafelski.com/work-with-me

ABOUT THE AUTHOR

Dr. Emy Tafelski is a soul guide and self-proclaimed badass spiritual rebel. She's on a mission to guide humans home to their true essence so that they can feel free, powerful, and confident. She truly believes authenticity is the magical elixir that can heal the world.

Dr. Tafelski's venture, which began in the realms of traditional therapy, has evolved into a blend of spirituality and integrative health, informed by her Ph.D. in psychology with a concentration in Consciousness, Spirituality, and Integrative Health. This evolution departs from conventional therapy, delving deeper into the soul for transformational healing. Her major offering is the comprehensive "Soul Weaving Experience," a custom, multi-day journey tailored to individual needs, challenges, and aspirations, with time spent releasing what doesn't serve and reclaiming personal power and confidence.

Dr. Tafelski's goal transcends individual healing; she aims to dismantle the patriarchal chains that restrict authentic self-expression across genders. By fostering unapologetic authenticity, she envisions a world where everyone can embrace their true selves, leading to a more healed and harmonious society.

As for the future, Emy is fully dedicated to her current path. This recent evolution of her practice represents a career and a calling—one she pursues with unwavering passion and commitment. Her work is more than a service; it's a movement toward a world where authenticity is accepted and celebrated.

She lives in St. Pete, Florida (though she's a native Jersey girl who still misses her pizza, but not winter), and when she's not out riding her motorcycle, she's at home chilling with her husband and their two cats, Cleo and Jellybean. You might also find her DMing the family game of Dungeons & Dragons for her adult stepdaughters, their partners, and her husband. Their game has magical cats because everywhere should have magical cats.

She's been heavily engaged in the game of trying to beat the Instagram algorithm at www.instagram.com/emytafelski.

She loves to write stories in weekly emails to her newsletter sub-scribers, where she models imperfection and healing. Get signed up by joining the free five-day Soulful Spark Email Challenge here: emytafelski.ck.page/spark.

www.ingramcontent.com/pod-product-compliance
Lightning Source LLC
Chambersburg PA
CBHW060540130626
46553CB00002B/834

9 798990 095670